INNER

The nature of belief in the inner city

C.S.LEWIS
CENTRE

INNER CITY GOD

The nature of belief in the inner city

Geoffrey Ahern
and
Grace Davie

Hodder & Stoughton
LONDON SYDNEY AUCKLAND TORONTO

British Library Cataloguing in Publication Data

Ahern, Geoffrey
  Inner city God: the nature of belief in
  the inner city.
  1. Church of England   2. Church and social
  problems—England   3. England—Social
  conditions—20th century
  I. Title   II. Davie, Grace
  261.1′0942   BX5131.2
  ISBN 0 340 40738 7

CONTENTS

Part Two:
'I do believe in Christmas'
White working-class people and
Anglican clergy in inner-city London

FOREWORD

I was brought up with a jolt when my description of parts of inner-city Liverpool as secularised was contradicted. Unchurched they certainly were, but they were rich in feelings after God, especially at moments like birth, marriage and death, values associated with Jesus Christ, superstitions about fate, and confidence about what constitutes hypocrisy. Grace Davie examines the different strands of common religion. Geoffrey Ahern's enquiry allows us to savour the experiences and attitudes of 'us' and 'them' in East London. Clergy and lay people who are concerned about the life of the church in urban priority areas and who take time with this study will ask themselves important questions about the appropriateness of our language, lifestyle and methods of decision-making.

Those who want to get beneath the surface of opinion polls, which report that 70% of people in Britain believe in God, will find a more complex web than they expect. Among the factors will be upbringing, responses to deprivation, the memories of a small community, and the media's reinforcing reflections of religion. For example, I have been intrigued by how many urban people have told me of their evacuation to the country as children in 1939. That rural experience seems frequently to have left an imprint associated with God.

I found this an honest attempt to examine religious attitudes in urban areas. It doesn't take long to discover that the great majority of urban working-class people in Europe and Britain are alienated from the institution of the church – whatever church – as they are from all institutions. We church people would do well to look hard at the uneasy and erratic relationship that many urban dwellers have with the church.

Many clergy and lay people are tempted to cut the knot which holds them in this ambivalent and demanding relationship. I well understand their uneasy conscience in asking people to make great promises in the baptism service. The tidy church, like a fortress with a moat round it, releases us from this confusing contact. But members of such a tidy church are soon asking how they can make contact with their neighbours. I believe it would be the greatest mistake for the Church of England, embedded as it is in so much of the fabric of the country, to want to sharpen all its blurred edges. We need all manner of stepping stones, if we are to meet people where they are. We ignore natural religion at our peril. A particular dread of mine is that those who feel themselves excluded from successful, organised life come to see the church as one more authority which insists that they must say the right words and fill in the right forms, before we will respond to what they want for their child.

I hope too that this book, published under the auspices of the C. S. Lewis Centre for the Study of Religion and Modernity, may be an encouragement to those who feel that their ministry is a failure. It shows how unreal are many of our yardsticks of success. The Centre's work will no doubt in due course point out other areas too where the church perceives its role one way and people in the neighbourhood see it very differently. For instance, on the Archbishop of Canterbury's Commission on Urban Priority Areas we realised in our visits that there are other models of success. The crowded church with individuals going off to their private and family interests has much to learn from many of the inner-city churches we saw; often there were small numbers, but their strong sense of belonging to one another and their commitment to join in serving the needs of a hurt community often seemed to us a true reflection of Jesus, the Servant of the Lord.

David Sheppard
Bishop of Liverpool

THE C. S. LEWIS CENTRE

The C. S. Lewis Centre for the Study of Religion and Modernity is a Christian research organisation working in partnership with Hodder and Stoughton to publish thought-provoking material concerning the relationship between the Christian faith and the modern world. Following C. S. Lewis's example, it is the Centre's deliberate policy to reach a broad market, speaking to 'everyman' in an intelligent and informed way, and responding to the challenge presented to orthodox belief by the secular culture of our contemporary society.

GENERAL INTRODUCTION

The C. S. Lewis Centre is pleased to bring together two important sociological studies on religious belief in the inner cities. In the wake of the Archbishop of Canterbury's Commission on Urban Priority Areas (*Faith In The City*), it is clear just how much work is needed in understanding the nature of inner-city life. Research is cumulative, and the present book is not intended to be a final word but rather a useful contribution to both understanding and combating the 'secularisation' of the urban areas of our modern cities.

It is wise to put the word 'secularisation' in inverted commas, because our cities are only secularised in the sense that we see a steady decline in religious attendance at church. This is not good news for Christianity, and certainly not for Christian orthodoxy, but religiosity itself – however vaguely experienced and poorly expressed – clearly abounds. Perhaps the central question for the Christian churches is, 'How do we tap this latent religion?' It follows, of course, that a vague religiosity may be tapped by New Religious Movements or other world religions, and so religiosity in itself is not necessarily a positive thing from a Christian viewpoint.

Both Dr Davie's and Dr Ahern's studies deal with this issue of latent or 'implicit' religion and seek to relate it to institutional Christianity. Grace Davie's study is a theoretical overview of the sociological approaches and literature relevant to the question of religious belief in the city. Such an overview is a useful introduction to the sociological debate concerning the complex phenomenon we call secularisation. Written in clear non-jargonised English, it will not only be welcomed by students of the sociology of religion but by the clergy and Christian workers ministering in the inner city.

A major and, it seems to me, justified complaint against sociology is that it is written in a language of vehement obscurity that benefits nobody but sociologists. On the other hand, when sociologists do venture out from behind their ivory towers they are usually accused of being too biased, or incapable of being 'value-free'. I think it true to say that we have come a long way from the nineteenth century, when Auguste Comte was of the opinion that sociology was the 'queen of the sciences'. No sociologist worth their salt these days makes sweeping claims for the superiority of their discipline over all others. The fact that few attempts are made to insist that sociology is as scientific as physics has led to a proper modesty.

Grace Davie's study is both modest and significant because she has provided a tool for understanding the nature of religion in the inner city that can be grasped by those engaged in mission and pastoral care. Her study is not designed specifically for clergy, but her overview of the academic literature is both timely and instructive.

What I think highlights the usefulness of her study is to see it in concert with Geoffrey Ahern's empirical research in the East End of London. His study can rightly be called modest: it is a small-scale qualitative analysis of attitudes towards the established church by indigenous East Enders. This is contrasted with a brief section on the problems as seen from the perspective of the clergy.

To call Geoffrey Ahern's study 'modest' needs unpacking a little. Large-scale social surveys of religious belief (such as Dr Robert Towler's seminal research in Leeds for example) are useful methods of investigation, but you have to pay a price: depth and quality are sacrificed for breadth and quantity. While small-scale qualitative analyses sacrifice the 'hard' data made possible by large-scale and numerical studies, they gain in digging below the surface and revealing the texture of religious feeling and experience which surveys miss altogether. At least qualitative studies do gain if they are handled by experienced and artful investigators. In this respect the C. S. Lewis Centre has good cause to thank Dr Ahern, whose expertise in this area is already ably demonstrated by his work in interviewing anthroposophists (*The Sun at Midnight*, Aquaria Press 1984), and Christian laypersons and their attitude to the Holy Trinity (a C. S. Lewis Centre mimeographed publication submitted to the British Council of Churches commission on the Trinity).

Geoffrey Ahern's paper is modest in another sense. There was not enough money to extend the study. Very few published works 'come clean' and admit this, but it is a fact of life that research is partly determined by the depth of the coffers. The C. S. Lewis Centre is grateful to the Christian Evidence Society, who commissioned this work, but they would be the first to admit that Dr Ahern's investigation begs to be continued by further researchers.

Such work is indeed now continuing. Just as our studies add pieces of the jigsaw to the overall picture of religion in the inner city, so further research is making that picture a little clearer. An important project is underway through the joint auspices of the Evangelical Coalition for Urban Mission and the British Church Growth Association.

As we hope that the present study will be read both by Christians interested in working in the inner city and by sociologists of religion, we must be clear in what sense *Inner City God* represents, if at all, a committed Christian approach. In order to answer that question we need to understand something of the nature of the C. S. Lewis Centre.

The Centre is an orthodox Christian research organisation that studies religion in the modern world. Such studies are of two kinds. Firstly, committed – and sometimes confrontational – attacks upon the evils, as we see

14

INNER CITY GOD

them, of modernity. This commitment stems from a broad Christian and trinitarian orthodoxy that is concerned in particular with the ideologies – the 'modernisms' – of modernity. But we cannot always be confronting modernity; sometimes we have to stand back and seek to understand it. So our second mode of study can rightly be called 'value-free' in the sense that we investigate the nature of advanced industrial societies according to the canons of academic enquiry. If that enquiry is scientific by nature, or even quasi-scientific, then it follows that confrontation and Christian commitment do not disappear, but they do take a back seat.

Inner City God clearly belongs to the second mode of investigation. The inner city is a feature of advanced industrial societies in both Europe and North America. As societies develop, we see a once prosperous urban city-dweller moving outwards to the suburbs, outer suburbs, and dormitory towns in ever-increasing concentric circles. The urban city in turn becomes the home of the migrant and immigrant worker. Often housing is private tenancy (the landlord having decamped outside the city) or public housing. As the new migrant workers move into the (so often) decaying housing, they conflict with the indigenous working-class communities – or rather broken and scattered communities – that were too poor or too weary to move out to the suburbs.

It would be a mistake to be too romantic and nostalgic about these communities. There is no evidence that they were ever deeply attached to churchgoing, and a hundred years or more ago even those Anglican clergy such as F. D. Maurice and Charles Kingsley who tried so hard to reach them through their Christian socialism found that the going was hard. Edward Denison, son of a bishop and once described as 'Brother of the Poor', had this to say of the East End:

Now about this East of London. What is so bad in it, is not what 'jumps at the eyes' as the French say. No; this summer there is not so much actual suffering for want of food, nor from sickness. What is so bad is the habitual condition of this mass of humanity – its uniform mean level, the absence of anything more civilizing than a grinding organ to raise the ideas beyond the daily bread and beer, the utter want of education, the complete indifference of religion, with the fruits of all this, viz., improvidence, dirt, and their secondaries, crime and disease . . . (cited in K. de Schweinitz, *England's Road to Social Security*, Perpetua 1961, p. 145).

Conversely, we may wonder if the middle-class attitudes of Victorian gentlemen who so believed in progress through education and the 'civilising' values ever really entered into the conditions of the poor. There was empathy, but not exactly solidarity. In this respect we may legitimately wonder if Anglican clergymen still find the cultural gap too wide to close. But we must beware of cynicism. In the first place it really was the case that godly men, often from the gentry and with both Catholic and socialist views, actually did live among people in the inner city. Anglo-Catholicism, for example, became truly embedded in the East End one hundred years ago (though it is somewhat adrift now). It was also the case that however hard and harsh life was in the inner cities communities really did exist, and they thrived despite the growth of urbanism. Even in the early 1960s community was alive in the East End (M. Young and P. Willmott, *Family and Kinship in East London*, Pelican 1962).

Both religion and community are alive today in the inner city, but they seem to be thriving more in immigrant populations than among the indigenous groups. Geoffrey Ahern's concentration on the white working class is not due to a white bias, but because it is there that we see the greatest erosion of both community and Christian religion. Anglican clergy must look at the Seventh Day Adventism and Pentecostalism of West Indians with barely disguised envy!

And it may very well be that the sectarians have a lesson to teach us all: If you cannot implant a church through natural community, then you must create your own community – and church – through voluntary association. It is significant that the house church movement is now beginning to make inroads into the inner city. In South London, for example, the West Indian leader Philip Mohbair and the 'Restorationist' team led by David Tomlinson are beginning to form a network of churches and fellowships in the heart of the urban areas. The white middle-class charismatic movement has so far had little impact on the inner city, but one of its leaders, Douglas McBain, has moved into the inner city in order to coordinate and stimulate working-class renewal groups.

These experiments are interesting precisely because they have bypassed the usual institutional structures. This has the advantage of not being seen as a 'them' religion. Base communities have similar advantages. But for the moment they remain 'experiments in faith'. Perhaps this reflects the difference between the established church and newer forms of religious organisation. The latter experiment by missioning, while the former set up Archbishops' commissions! In fact this is not fair: the Church of England is doing both these things, and it would be foolish to pretend that we do not need research when it is so clear that we are still uninformed about inner-city life.

The pressures of modernity hit the poor in the inner cities harder than anyone else: unemployment is higher, education is of an inferior standard (or at least has fewer resources), racism is rampant, and housing is dilapidated. It is surely a witness to the human spirit that religiosity has survived. But this is not good news for the Christian churches unless the Christian faith can be integrated into the lives and reality of urban existence. This is not a question of making the gospel relevant. Whenever intellectuals talk of making the gospel relevant they mean scaling it down to fit some romantic vision they have of the modern man. That is why I believe that Geoffrey Ahern is right to insist that abstract social-issues religion leaves the working man cold. What men, and women want, is hope. This, as Bishop Leslie Newbigin has realised, is the great crisis of modernity (*The Other Side of 84*, BCC 1983).

Just as I have allowed my values to show in this introduction, so also do Grace Davie and Geoffrey Ahern allow themselves a break from their 'disinterested' role as social observers and show a little of their own feelings. As Grace Davie is a Christian and Geoffrey Ahern is an agnostic, it is not surprising that Dr Ahern is perhaps less optimistic than Dr Davie. Neither of their views necessarily reflects the views of the C. S. Lewis Centre, but we are pleased that they were able to make some positive suggestions in this complex and difficult area for Church mission. Geoffrey Ahern's recommendations are made on the basis of reflection and involvement with the study in the East End. They are not in any way, however, to be read as directly stemming from the data itself. In this respect the study stands as an independent and objective sociological investigation.

The C. S. Lewis Centre would like to thank Professor David Martin for his help in advising us at the preliminary stages of the investigations. It was he who first suggested that we should publish Grace Davie's and Geoffrey Ahern's studies together.

Andrew Walker
The C. S. Lewis Centre for the Study
of Religion and Modernity
London 1987

Part One

The nature of belief in the inner city

by

Grace Davie

Research commissioned by the Archbishop of
Canterbury's Commission on Urban Priority Areas

ACKNOWLEDGMENTS

The following paper was initially requested by the Archbishop of Canterbury's Commission on Urban Priority Areas. I am grateful to the Commission both for the opportunity to undertake this piece of work and for their subsequent encouragement to publish the paper. I am particularly indebted to those members of the Commission and their advisors who took considerable time and trouble to discuss the issues with me. It was Graham Howes who both suggested the project to me and, as it were, set me on my way.

That the original paper should now appear in its present form is largely due to Dr Andrew Walker, who suggested publishing my review of the academic literature in the field of common or implicit religion alongside Dr Geoffrey Ahern's empirical work in the same area.

Many others have helped me to understand the nature of belief and its implications for the churches' ministry, not least those with extensive first-hand experience of the inner city; to them is due my respect as well as my thanks. From a more academic perspective, I discussed the project with a number of people committed to the study of belief; I must particularly mention Canon Edward Bailey, who masterminds the Network for the Study of Implicit Religion, and those involved in the project on 'Conventional religion and common religion in Leeds' directed by Dr Robert Towler. In addition, Dr Towler gave permission for me to quote extensively from the Religious Research Papers of the Department of Sociology at the University of Leeds.

Finally, I am grateful to Canon Wesley Carr, who gave me valuable comments on the original draft of the paper, and to R. T. Davies, who eliminated my worst stylistic faults. I alone am responsible for what remains.

Grace Davie

INTRODUCTION

The following chapters were initially written for the Archbishop of Canterbury's Commission on Urban Priority Areas. On the Commission's behalf I was asked to review the sociological literature concerned with the nature of belief in Britain today, and to consider the conclusions of this review with respect to the terms of reference of the Archbishop's Commission.[1] More particularly, the Commission was asking whether the quality or nature of belief in itself rendered the churches' task more difficult in urban priority areas, and wanted to know if sociologists had any evidence on this question one way or the other. I was also encouraged to suggest ways in which my conclusions could have practical application.

The Commission's request for a review of literature accounts for the rather curious shape of this piece of work. Though not much more than a long essay, it contains a disproportionate number of footnotes and appendices. In the main the footnotes cover the bibliographical references to the sociological literature on the nature of belief, and the first two appendices review particular approaches to this field of enquiry. The chapters themselves provide a framework in which to consider this material. The third appendix, on the relationship of belief to belonging, raises a specific question put to me by the Commission. Clearly it relates to the paper as a whole, but considers the subject from a rather particular perspective; it is, however, an unavoidable subject for those trying to understand the dynamics of ministry.

In some ways the task given to me by the Commission was closely circumscribed, and fed into a specific part of their work; the principal findings of my review were summarised in the third chapter of *Faith in the City*. In other ways the task proved wide-ranging, in that the 'nature of belief' is not easily defined as a subject and rather inevitably it spreads into many other areas of study. In consequence, careful definition of the problem takes up much of the first part of the paper. Within this, a number of sociological approaches to implicit or common religion[2] are outlined and their advantages and disadvantages commented on, bearing in mind the particular terms of reference of the Archbishop's Commission.

The second chapter begins to construct the framework which I feel to be fundamental to the understanding of this material; that is, the need to consider people's religious ideas within the context in which they occur. It should be said at once that I do not mean by this any kind of rigid determinism whereby beliefs become dependent on a particular social or economic situation. What I do want to stress is that belief cannot exist apart from its context (historical, social or cultural) and that an awareness of this context is essential to a proper understanding of what is going on.

For example, chapter two begins to explore the question of belief with reference to aspects of the secularisation debate, in order to highlight the particular stresses experienced in contemporary Britain. It should not be assumed that what obtains in Britain in this respect is necessarily the same as in any other country, even if we limit the discussion to Western Christianity or indeed to Western Europe. However, the approach concerns more than national patterns; context, after all, can be visualised at many levels – international, national, regional and so on, right down to very local aspects, even within one city. Each of these may be of importance regarding the nature of an individual's religious ideas.

If the secularisation debate introduces the more wide-ranging of these contexts, the more detailed questions referred to me by the Commission asked for comment concerning the more local. In particular, does the nature of belief relate in any way to a certain type of urban neighbourhood? The third chapter will tackle this aspect of the question, which proved in fact to be considerably more complex than the Commission's original enquiry implied. Indeed the complexity of the whole issue is the predominant conclusion; there are no easy answers to understanding the nature of belief. But some lines of enquiry are more helpful than others, and as a conclusion to this chapter various sociological approaches to the nature of belief are outlined. These at least provide a way into the issues involved, even if the answers that emerge are not always clear cut.

A final part of the paper will try to relate the conclusions regarding the nature of belief in areas of economic deprivation to the more practical task of the churches that minister in those parts of our cities. In order to do this, I explore further the very intricate relationship between conventional, or institutionalised, religion and common religion. What seem to emerge are a number of variations in this relationship; moreover these variations are associated with different parts of our society. This conclusion has considerable implications for those whose job involves not only the maintenance of the church in an urban priority area but also its mission. I hope very much that the conclusions reached will in the main encourage those who take responsibility for this difficult task; in particular, I suggest that too great a preoccupation with the conventional indicators of success is unnecessarily depressing. It seems that attitudes within the church may be as much to blame for a sense of failure as the nature of belief outside it.

This point may need a little clarification. If, in trying to understand the situation better, I have at times been critical of church structures and have suggested that per-

sisting with certain policies is more of a hindrance than a
help, I do not wish to imply that the solution lies in doing
away with these structures. Indeed, I underline the point
that the Church of England is an institution with a long and
specific history which cannot be unpicked, even if we
should want to do so. Moreover, tearing down structures is
both expensive and time-consuming; it rarely achieves the
aims envisaged and often has unexpected and rather negative results. A more realistic way forward, it seems to me, is
an honest appraisal of the situation – including an ack-
nowledgment of the very real problems there are – and
then a commitment to work as flexibly as possible within
the framework that we have. Of course this does not
preclude modification of ecclesiastical structures – for
example, the redefinition of out-of-date parish or denominational boundaries, or indeed the reconsideration of the
way in which we assess success. (This kind of modification
goes on all the time, informally as well as formally.) The
stress, though, lies in finding new ways forward within the
limits set by the past, rather than rejecting the past altogether. For instance, in an urban priority area, one very
obvious limit set by the past is the lack of regular contact
between most individuals and the institutional church; this
is a state of affairs that has existed for several generations.
It seems more sensible to accept this limitation and to work
within it than to assume any great change of heart within
the near future.

Just how much flexibility the church can permit itself is
nevertheless a difficult question. Indeed, it raises a whole
series of wider issues which derive from the inevitable
tension between the essential catholicity of the Christian
gospel and the local context in which this is worked out.
This complex problem has many aspects; the nature of
belief is only one of them. On the other hand, it may be that
considering the nature of belief and its implications for
ministry in an urban priority area focuses this tension more
acutely than other areas of the church's work. For

example, just how far can belief be considered in any way Christian if there is no real contact with the church? How far and in what ways can you adapt liturgy to suit a particular subculture? How much freedom is the individual minister to have in the interpretation of his role? In what ways can he minister effectively to people who are reluctant to attend services? Furthermore, it is likely that at least some of these questions are becoming more urgent, rather than less, in contemporary Britain, in that churchgoing is clearly diminishing throughout our society. Despite the very real dilemmas which emerge in thinking through these issues, there may therefore be a long-term gain; an awareness sharpened by difficult circumstances can help the church as a whole to think more clearly.

One or two further preliminaries concern the sources available to me.

Most of the material for the following paper comes from the sociological literature related to studies of both conventional and common religion, with a particular emphasis on the latter. It is, however, almost entirely limited to the material available in this country, with a few references to work pursued in the United States. Yet the questions put to me are of wider significance, and it is important to realise that there is an extensive European literature in this area which could provide fruitful lines of enquiry.

A second point is also important: I have reviewed the literature in so far as I could find it. In the case of the academic literature, this was relatively straightforward; the work is either published or reference can be found in the appropriate bibliographies.[3] I became increasingly aware, however, of a number of rather different studies relevant to this theme. These are often locally based initiatives prepared within a particular diocese or for a specific congregation; for the most part they exist in the form of typescripts with limited circulation and to which there is no organised access. Clearly such studies vary a great deal in quality, and care is needed in their interpretation. On the other hand, they could prove a rich seam of evidence if made more widely available. The ones that I have cited are those which I have stumbled across; I suspect that there are many more.

There is another aspect to this problem of scope. In view of the particular questions put to me by the Commission, I have for the most part concentrated on the principal church groupings of this country, though there are a few references to minority groups in the appendix on believing and belonging. But it is clear that the approach outlined in this paper could be applied to religious beliefs quite different from those embodied in Western Christianity; comparative study could well point up significant features within our own situation and the particular qualities of Christianity. For example, in other religions, very different patterns may emerge with respect to the relationship between context and belief or between institutionalised practice and more diffused beliefs.

To return to the question of sources, I have – in addition to reviewing the literature – discussed with a wide variety of people the conclusions that seemed to emerge. Both academics and those whose work centres on areas associated with economic deprivation were consulted. Inevitably, a rather disproportionate number of the latter are working in Liverpool. This, as well as my own experience of such an atypical city, is bound to colour my thinking to some degree, though the more general conclusions of the paper remain, I hope, unaffected. Indeed, one of the most important of these conclusions is the significance of a very immediate context for understanding religious belief; the principle therefore remains the same, though the local application will always be different.

Finally, it is important to clarify the relationship of my paper both to the report of the Archbishop's Commission and to Geoffrey Ahern's paper. With respect to the former, I have already indicated that my conclusions fed into one rather specific aspect of this report. I have, though, been struck by a number of other points of contact with the report, and where appropriate I have underlined these in the footnotes. A good example of this would be the stress of the Commission on the importance of the local community both as an indicator of social health and as an effective level for the churches' action. My own conclusions reinforced this view.

Dr Ahern's study was completed after I had submitted my paper to the Commission. His empirical findings are, however, of considerable significance to my own conclusions, and in a number of cases I have drawn attention to this. That we do not always interpret this intricate material in the same way is perhaps an indication of its complexity and the need for the utmost care in evaluating such findings. There are indeed no easy answers.

1

SOCIOLOGICAL APPROACHES TO
THE NATURE OF BELIEF

Sociologists of religion have come some way since they were considered – in David Martin's phrase – as 'academic deviants living by a non-existent subject'. One reason for this gain in respectability has been their move away from the study of institutional religion (generally agreed to be of declining importance in our society) to a much wider concern with some of the problems facing contemporary societies and those who live in them. For example: if religious beliefs as traditionally defined gave meaning to life and the vicissitudes experienced therein, what has replaced such beliefs for modern man – still faced with much the same problems, though their particular expression may alter? Or, secondly, what is likely to be the consequence for society if traditional beliefs about man's destiny are discarded and nothing is found to replace them?

The importance of such questions is widely recognised and clearly sociologists are right to be concerned with them. However, a swing in emphasis of such magnitude brings problems of its own, not least that of definition or delineation of the area in question. And if sociologists are agreed that the study of 'religion' should include more than observations about its conventional or institutional practice, they are certainly not clear about the new frame of reference that is to replace this. Hence the plethora of terms that have emerged in the attempt to locate what exactly is the focus of their enquiries.[1] A full discussion of this question is beyond the scope of this paper, but some guidelines may be helpful none the less.

Richard Toon's introductory study to the Leeds enquiry into conventional and common religion gives a very clear and relatively short outline of the issues involved in this question.[2] From his discussion, four 'types' of religion emerge: conventional religion, common religion, invisible religion and surrogate religion. Toon relates them all to two fundamental dimensions: organised/non-organised and supernatural/empirical. He represents his scheme diagrammatically:

Dimensions of the definition of religion

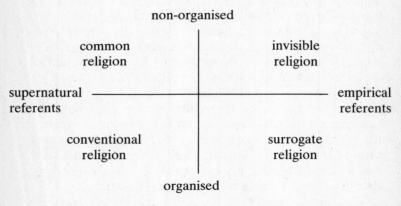

For example, with reference to the lower half of the diagram, if conventional religion includes organised activities that have some reference to the supernatural, surrogate religion covers the kind of all-absorbing activity often seen as an equivalent to organised religion, but without supernatural referents. Football is often quoted in this instance.

It is, however, the non-organised half of the diagram that

is most relevant to more broadly based sociological studies. In fact the important point to grasp from Toon's analysis is that he has, together with those who have worked with him, clearly picked out an area which 'does not go beyond the common understanding of what counts as religion, and yet which includes more than simply "church-orientated religion"'[3]; that is, an area which includes reference to the supernatural but spreads beyond organised religion. This relates to the segment of the diagram labelled as 'common religion', and takes up the definition first proposed by Robert Towler in his earlier work in Leeds.[4] An outline of what is meant by this phrase, the content of common religious themes, the possible sources of information about these, and the methodological problems associated with its study will form the basis of this part of my report.

However, in order to appreciate this emphasis fully it is first necessary to consider briefly those who have a wider approach to the subject and who follow Thomas Luckmann's definition of natural or invisible religion, which refers to 'a system of symbolic meaning in which there is no reference to the supernatural';[5] nor (if we go back to the diagram) is this 'religion' organised in any way. Rather, the exponents of this type of approach are looking for what – in everyday language – makes people tick. What are their frames of reference and wherein do they find meaning for life?

Such an approach is clearly important to our understanding of society and, furthermore, can be applied at any level; for as well as asking questions about the individual, the same can be asked of groups, organisations, communities and even nations. This latter point is helpful because it stresses the fact that what is meaningful for one sector of society may not be so for another (a point to which we shall return in later chapters). On the other hand, the rather inclusive notion that every aspect of ordinary life, at any level, may have religious meaning is not, on the whole, all that useful in practical terms. An inability to see the wood for the trees is a likely consequence of following this approach too far, for if 'religious' meanings are potentially everywhere, how do we draw these together into something we can recognise and talk about? A further difficulty arises in that the use of the label 'religious' becomes very subjective: what one researcher may see as a meaningful focus of society, another may not; it is therefore likely that we shall learn more about the researchers than the society that they are studying.

For these reasons – but at the same time extracting the more helpful emphases from Luckmann's approach – I have chosen to use in the main the term 'common religion' and the definition of this that was first outlined by Towler and then taken up by all of those associated with the Leeds project on common religion. Indeed, one of the greatest merits of the Leeds enquiry is the consistency in its use of terms and exactness of concepts, thus enabling comparative work of a cumulative nature. In this field of study these are major advantages.

Towler defines common religion as 'those beliefs and practices of an overtly religious nature which are not under the domination of a prevailing religious institution'.[6] What then does this category include in our society? The scope of this subject is well illustrated by the range and variety within the interview schedule used for the Leeds investigation. As well as asking about more conventional religious adherence and activity, the questionnaire covers the paranormal, fortune telling, fate and destiny, the existence of God, life after death, ghosts, spiritual experiences, prayer and meditation, luck and superstition.[7]

Common religion clearly includes a wide area of human experience; moreover, this is an area which has a curious relationship to more conventional religion. For example, within common religion there are some ideas which relate quite closely to the church's teaching, but there are others which do not: a readiness to turn to the churches in connection with specific events in life or to consult the churches' personnel in times of need may well exist along-side belief in the power of fate or in ghosts and other aspects of the paranormal.

A second – related – point is also important. Common religion is by nature thematic and not systematic; it is made up of a large number of separate elements which do not necessarily form a coherent whole. An individual may well contradict himself in the course of an interview about his beliefs. Such inconsistencies are a long way from the creative tensions of systematic theology; rather they are the 'comfortable contradictions'[8] of everyday thought – often barely perceived by the individual in question, but none the less very much part of his 'religious' outlook.

It is, however, important to note that some commentators have been critical of the concept of common religion on precisely these points. It is felt that the concept encompasses too much and blurs distinctions between beliefs that derive, however remotely, from official religion and those which are little more than magic or superstition. An intermediate term such as 'customary religion' is suggested to cover the sort of beliefs which have at least some relation to the official teaching, even if these are no longer effectively controlled by the churches. How far such beliefs are distinguished in practice from the wider area of superstition or even the remnants of pre-Christian religion would seem to be the crucial question in deciding between these two sociological approaches. Unequivocal answers to this kind of question are, however, unlikely; in fact, it seems that the results that emerge may depend to a considerable extent upon the particular groups selected for this kind of study.[9] Clearly this is an area where further research is necessary.

Having achieved at least some agreement on the area to be studied, how then does the sociologist proceed? What are his possible sources of information about this rather confused subject and how does he get the most from them?

The question of sources, their advantages and disadvantages, is very adequately dealt with by Towler himself in his paper 'Conventional and Common Religion in Great Britain'.[10] Briefly, these include studies of folklore, historical work, cultural studies, Gorer's analysis of national character, psychological and anthropological approaches to the question as well as sociological investigation *per se*; and only after each of these has been assessed does Towler go on to consider various empirical studies, including his own work in Leeds. Examples of all these approaches are given in the notes.[11] It can be seen at once that many disciplines can contribute to our knowledge about common religion or popular belief, and each approach will present a certain emphasis. When these are taken together, a more accurate picture begins to emerge. For example, the folklorists and historians make it clear that common religion has always existed alongside orthodoxy – this is not something new to the twentieth century;[12] the anthropologists (whether speaking about primitive countries or applying their approach to communities within our own country) demonstrate the importance of seeing common religion within a particular social or cultural context – as one part of a complex whole; and the psychologists look at the problem from the point of view of the individual rather than the group – why, for example, do people maintain views for which there appears to be no rational basis (what psychological mechanisms come into play)?

Having absorbed this kind of information, a sociologist who wishes to go further – to attempt to be more precise about what proportion of people believe, what exactly is the content of their beliefs, and how these fit into other aspects of their life, etc. – has to decide what method he will adopt to research this. Broadly speaking, he will have to choose between two major approaches, that is a survey of some kind or participant observation. Obviously each approach will contribute complementary material to an overall picture, and perhaps an ideal study would combine the two.[13] Similarly, the difficulties involved are complementary; where a survey – however sophisticated – is open to criticism as being unsympathetic to the nature of the material being elicited (many common religion themes are by definition almost inarticulate), participant observers run the risk of being too subjective or too impressionistic.[14] In the latter case the researcher's frame of reference is clearly paramount; while some researchers can write of the city with no mention of religion at all, others can see religious meanings as a pervasive force in a community's life. What does seem to emerge as a general pattern is the relative strength of religious themes in studies of rural communities and the lack of them in an urban context. It would be interesting to investigate how much of this difference may be accounted for by the expectations of the observer concerned.[15]

Given these difficulties and shortcomings, what kind of results emerge in this field? A brief outline of some of these, with a number of references for further information, will provide a framework for subsequent chapters.

A large number of studies took place in the years following the Second World War. These are gathered together by David Martin in his *Sociology of English Religion* (chapter 3), though reference to the originals, especially Gorer's study and Mass Observation's *Puzzled People*, will flesh out the bare bones of his summary.[16] On one point all agree: the British are by a considerable majority a believing people. For example, Mass Observation found that four out of five women and two out of three men 'give at least verbal assent to the possibility of there being a God, and most of the rest express doubt rather than disbelief. Uncompromising disbelievers in a Deity amount to one in twenty.'[17] However, it is also clear that such views are not uniformly distributed through society, and this unevenness is related not only to sex but also to age and geographical area; compared with these factors, social class differences are less significant.[18] On the other hand, side by side with this fairly widespread acceptance of the idea of a non-empirical aspect to life – the sense that this world is in some way penultimate – there is a noticeable reluctance to express such beliefs by orthodox churchgoing, and here social class does have a marked effect in addition to sex, age and geographical differences. On this point, Gorer sums up his findings as follows:

> On the basis of these figures a married working class man living in London or Birmingham and their conurbations is unlikely to make any public profession of religion; women, particularly the unmarried or widowed, the very young, members of the upper middle and middle classes, and the inhabitants of the small towns and villages are much more likely to be at least intermittent church-goers.[19]

The enquiries continue through a varied range of questions, revealing a high incidence of private prayer (though again not by any means always related to churchgoing), much sympathy for religious education, a fair amount of antipathy towards organised religion and a truly wonderful confusion of doctrine. It is not difficult to see how elements of common religion antithetical to Christianity can become incorporated into such beliefs, for it seems that orthodox Christian theology plays little part in the everyday thinking of our nation.[20]

How far do these results hold some thirty to forty years later? The Leeds enquiry was set up with the intention – among other things – of providing a significant body of empirical material on popular religion in this country; this material would provide answers to at least some of these questions. However, in order to place the Leeds work in its proper context Towler first reviews a number of complementary sociological studies, each of which has some bearing on this problem.[21] Among these, one stands out in particular – that of Nicholas Abercrombie and his colleagues – in that it begins to explore the relationship between the various elements in common religion. It is worth quoting at some length from their conclusion:

> The analysis in the section above suggests the tentative conclusion that religious belief, when not associated with active membership of a church, tends to be associated with superstitious belief while church attendance tends to be antithetical to superstition. Moreover, we have some evidence that for those people who do not go to church but yet say they are religious and pray often, religious belief has moved quite far from the orthodox church position and is really much closer to what would normally be called superstition.[22]

The fieldwork for this enquiry took place in Islington in 1968. Though limited in its scope, the rigour with which it was carried out has earned for the study a high reputation. It also includes the best 'quote' of the literature. When being probed about their belief in God, respondents were asked, 'Do you believe in a God who can change the course of events on earth?' To which one individual replied, 'No, just the ordinary one.'[23] Answers such as this begin to reveal the problems associated with this type of study, particularly for the less articulate respondent; we shall come back to this point. None the less, Abercrombie and his associates have tentatively disclosed relationships between different elements in common religion and the importance of enquiring further along these lines.

The Leeds study aimed to do precisely this, though the detailed results are still awaited.[24] However, the basic frequencies already published indicate that the figures collected by Gorer or Mass Observation seem, broadly speaking, to be still correct; that is, over 70% of the Leeds sample assented to questions about belief in God.[25] The expected differences obtain for men and women and for old and young; the analysis of the results against social class has yet to be done.

To a very large extent these findings are reinforced by the figures coming out of the European Values Study. In this enquiry 76% of British people – though largely an unchurched population – said they believed in God. On the other hand, questions about the ten commandments, about moral guidelines and about good and evil revealed considerable differences among the British, though distinctive patterns emerged.[26] The significance of these figures, and in particular their relevance to the churches' task, is discussed more fully in chapter four.

Before leaving this question, however, it is important to mention a major difference in context between postwar studies and those of the 1980s. This concerns the role of the media – and especially television – and its influence on both conventional and common religion, a factor that can hardly be ignored, though relatively little work has been done in this field. As an offshoot of the work at Leeds, Kim Knott has investigated in some detail the relationship between religion and the media. Her conclusions are of considerable interest: 'Not only does the contemporary religious situation have a bearing on the media portrayal of religion, but, conversely, the portrayal itself is responsible for helping to shape and reinforce popular religion and religiosity.'[27] This symbiotic relationship between these two aspects of our society is clearly a crucial one, for if television claims to be a mirror held up to life, it also 'fashions' religion to some extent. If this is the case, the attitudes and outlook of those responsible for the media become of great significance. It is important to ask whether these people are representative of the wider population with respect to their religious outlook, or whether they are more likely to form part of a rather atypical minority. This point is explored further by Dr Knott in her paper *Media Portrayals of Religion and their Reception.*[28] It is a question to which we shall return in the next chapter.

THE SECULARISATION DEBATE: THE BRITISH CONTEXT

Sociologists have focused much of their debate about religion and its significance around the notion that religious belief and practice seem to be of declining importance in contemporary society.[1] The secularisation debate is complex and wide-ranging, and much of it is clearly beyond the terms of reference of this paper.[2] The controversy does, however, provide a starting point from which we can begin to examine the British context in which the process of secularisation is taking place; it is this aspect that I want to stress in particular. The significance of the British context in this respect will be highlighted by comparing it to one or two other cultural situations.[3]

Because of the particular turn of historical events in Britain, we find ourselves in a society which – though unwilling to practise its religion in formal churchgoing – is by no means anti-religious in spirit. This relative tolerance towards religion pertains in almost all walks of life in Britain, but it is a state of affairs that cannot just be assumed. For example, a rather different pattern has emerged in Latin Europe, where the religious history is very different. Here the monolithic tendencies of Roman Catholicism permitted no Christian dissent for a very long time (Protestantism was ruthlessly persecuted); in consequence dissent tended to become anti-Christian as well as anti-Catholic. 'Secular' and 'revolutionary' were adjectives that came to be associated with one another, and anti-clericalism persisted as a political force until relatively recently.

The contrast between Britain and Latin Europe in this respect is fundamental; because of historical circumstances, religion in this country 'feels' quite different. Furthermore this difference can be illustrated in a number of ways, some of them very relevant to everyday life and thought. A good example of this is language use. The French notion of *laicité* and the associated adjective *laique* are very difficult to convey in English; yet more profound than the lack of vocabulary is the fact that our culture has no need of the concept – it does not fit into our consciousness. Similarly, within popular literature, the principal characters in the Italian Don Camillo stories (the Roman Catholic priest and his foil the Communist mayor) simply do not have English counterparts; theirs were rivalries that do not occur in our society. Instead we have had debates – often heated ones – about types of religion (in our case between different expressions of Christianity). In contrast, arguments about the rights of religion *per se* are not part of our way of life; there is no major cleavage in Britain associated with religion/anti-religion.

To fill in the picture a bit further, the American situation is different again; here not only does religious belief hold up well, but so too does religious practice.[4] Again, because of the nation's history, the American pattern permits 'religion to take on as many images as there are social faces' and a form of American Christianity can be found to fit almost every kind of social style. Indeed 'selections of religious style are made on an open market in accordance with variations of intimate personal biography'.[5] In consequence, the massive rejection of religion found among the continental working class just does not obtain in the United States. Britain stands somewhere between these extremes.

Given this picture of Britain as an intermediate type,

what then does 'believing in God' mean for British people? Does it always mean the same thing; do variations here relate to particular parts of the country or to particular economic or social circumstances, and what are the consequences for those ministering in such circumstances? These are the questions to which we must now turn, and at this point it will be necessary to scratch beneath the statistics provided by social surveys and lean more towards the evidence supplied by those observing at first hand the communities concerned.

However, before leaving the secularisation debate completely, it is worth pointing out one further area of study not so far mentioned. This is the work of the Alister Hardy Research Centre in Oxford and of the Religious Experience and Education Project in Nottingham. Both these are now under the direction of David Hay.[6] The patiently collected evidence of those working in this field points to an appreciable number of people who – if asked – will claim to have had a 'religious' experience of one kind or another. But by no means all of these people are churchgoers, and a number admitted to hiding such experiences for fear of appearing foolish. Religion is 'kept secret' in what is perceived as a hostile environment. Hay concludes:

> We would hypothesize that to chart the decline of the Western religious institution as the one true indicator of secularization may be to misrepresent what is going on. An alternative account, hinted at by our findings, is that religious interpretations of human experience are by no means disappearing. The fact that these theologies are unsophisticated, at times apparently naive and do not appear in official textbooks of religion, means that they are not easily visible to the investigator.[7]

A number of these points will re-emerge later on. At this stage, however, it seems that this kind of evidence gives us one more reason to wonder about the supposedly secular society in which we live. Could this in fact be a figment of imagination on the part of an atypical – but none the less influential – élite? It is clear that we should not underestimate the strength of religious currents in society merely because of their diffuse and unstructured nature. David Martin puts it as follows: 'Those who talk about secularization are generally either humanists or existentialist theologians. Whatever we are we are *not* a secular society, particularly if by that omnibus adjective we mean an increasing approximation of average thinking to the norms of natural and social science.'[8] Kim Knott's reference to those responsible for the media (page 40) is just one example of this more general point; hence perhaps the tendency of those involved in the broadcasting of religion on television to adjust the content of programmes to suit our supposedly scientific age and to accept rather uncritically an irreparable decline in religious institutions.

BELIEF IN A LOCAL CONTEXT

A general, if rather superficial, pattern should now be coming clear: we find in Britain a relatively large number of people who say that they believe in God but who are none the less reluctant to express this belief in churchgoing. However, the surveys reviewed in the second chapter have already hinted at differences in the distribution of belief and practice through society, and it is this question that must concern us now. Religious indicators of all kinds reflect differences between men and women, between young and old, and between different geographical locations; Gorer summarised these succinctly (page 38). The relationship between religion and social class is more problematic; whereas the relationship is straightforward enough with respect to religious practice, it is much less clear with respect to belief, and nonexistent in some of the less orthodox aspects of common religion.[1]

These statistical variations are undoubtedly important, and we need as much accurate information about such matters as is possible. However, having considered the problem with some care, I wonder if a whole series of more far-reaching questions lies beneath these statistics which it is equally important to draw out. For example, it may or may not be true that more or less people believe in God in a working class, or even in a deprived area, than in society in general, but in addition to any such numerical variations it is essential to ask questions about the nature of that belief.

For instance, how do different people think about the 'God' in whom they are supposed to believe? Do they think about him at all? What do they envisage as 'the church'? Does hostility to the church necessarily imply hostility to the idea of God? Moreover, considering the nature of belief in this kind of way leads in turn to another set of issues. These concern the acquisition, transmission and articulation of belief, and begin to raise questions about how people acquire and pass on their religious ideas. For example, what influence does their immediate context have on their thinking? How are beliefs handed on from generation to generation? How are they articulated, if at all? Probing along these lines is perhaps a better way to reveal significant differences within our society than merely counting heads; nuances emerge that are masked by statistics but which are of considerable importance to our understanding.[2]

The relationship between a social context and a particular cultural expression is, however, a complex one, and any kind of rigid determinism must be avoided; it is clear that not all people living in particular social or economic conditions think in the same terms. On the other hand, it seems to me very unlikely that different conditions of life do not colour people's thinking – and this includes their religious thinking – in any way at all, and it is this issue that we must consider first.

As an example of this approach, we can take one question in particular – how do people picture the God in whom they believe? What kinds of adjectives will they use to convey what they mean? Does the idea of judgment or love prevail; is God malign or benign? Social surveys are obviously of less help here;[3] rather, we must look for material in a number of sources to give at least an indication of the range of possibilities. (The following examples are not intended as comparisons one with another; rather they are chosen to illustrate the great variety of ideas that may be associated with God in people's minds.)

One extreme view, possibly more extreme than any that might occur in Britain, comes from Italy:

> For the typical peasant, God (or Christ, the terms are used interchangeably) is not a spirit of loving kindness or even of firm justice. He is a demanding and capricious overlord. He may not notice one at all. If He does, He may distribute bounty or catastrophe according to whim.
>
> Many think of God as a hostile, aggressive force who must be propitiated.[4]

Contrast this with some of the well-remembered lines of English hymns,

> Gentle Jesus meek and mild
> Look upon a little child,

or

> Loving shepherd of thy sheep
> Keep thy lamb, in safety keep,

and the question 'Do you believe in God?' is clearly a mere preliminary. Within the British context, the Leeds survey shows that in general more people – when faced with a list of suggested attributes of God – circle 'love', 'protector' or 'creator' rather than 'judge' or 'master';[5] on the other hand, such an image cannot just be assumed for everyone, and it is quite possible that extreme (or even relative) hardship may influence these choices.[6]

Interesting evidence for different pictures of God among poor people comes from a relatively new source; that of oral evidence taken from elderly people recalling experiences at the end of the last century.[7] In these particular interviews, two contrasting themes occur with some frequency:

> One is bitterness against, or total rejection of God, arising out of the experience of poverty generally, or from specific personal misfortunes; the other is trust in God, and turning to

him for strength in times of trouble. Both kinds of religious
response to poverty, deprivation and misfortune were quite
widespread . . .[8]

Furthermore, it seems that both types of reaction were
influenced by the conditions of life; existence was hard and
God was implicated in that hardship, whether positively or
negatively.

In parenthesis, further points of interest come from this
evidence: for example, people's reluctance to talk freely
about their personal beliefs, and their tendency to concentrate on more formal or factual matters;[9] the complexity
and ambivalence of many people's religious attitudes[10] and
the very different interpretations that can be put upon this
evidence, depending upon the outlook of the researcher.[11]
Indeed, not much seems to have changed; sociologists are
still confronting the same sorts of problems as they try to
dig beneath superficial impressions, and only very tentative
conclusions are possible. Bearing this in mind, it seems to
me likely that economic or social hardship probably does
colour the way in which people believe, but the precise
nature of the change cannot be predicted with any certainty. There is little contemporary evidence to help us on
this point.[12]

However, in addition to social or economic experiences,
an enormous number of other factors may have an influence on an individual's way of believing, and weighing
the relative strength of these factors will be a hazardous
business. In enumerating some of these, I hope that – if
nothing else – the complexity of the problem may be
emphasised. Distortion through oversimplification will not
help to clarify the issues in question.

Let us start with the broad outlines. Religious beliefs or
values have to some extent a universal aspect since they
deal with – or attempt to provide answers to – problems
posed by the condition of being human. Birth, death and
suffering are part of the process of life and are unavoidable

for every one of us in the long run, though suffering may of course vary in its forms and degrees. A. M. Greeley's thesis of the persistence of religion emphasises this universal theme; he concludes that religious questions are, if anything, becoming more pertinent, not less, in the contemporary world as human living becomes ever more complicated.[13] However, overlaying this emphasis on universality is an infinite variety of patterns, both between the major religious traditions and within them. Although our cities now house representatives of many world religions, I want to discuss this approach in the main within Western Christianity; it could, however, apply equally to other religious persuasions.

We have already seen that historical circumstances colour contemporary religious behaviour and that different patterns obtain in different countries, all of which lie within the Christian tradition. Within this framework, British people emerged as being on the whole favourably disposed towards religious ideas though reluctant to go to their various churches. There are, however, very marked regional differences within Britain in this respect, not least in the quite distinct religious traditions of Wales or Scotland. But even if we confine our discussions to England, it is clear that strong regional flavours persist, and beneath these regional variations lie quite contrasted ways of thinking. Moreover, this kind of analysis can be applied at a variety of levels. For example, the North West may have a particular religious identity in contrast, say, to the South West; on a very obvious level, the former has an unusually high number of Roman Catholics, the latter an important nonconformist population. But even within the North West there are distinct subcultures with respect to religious feeling. Liverpool and Wigan are good illustrations of this point. They are barely twenty miles apart, each has suffered economic decline, and both are part of the same Anglican diocese; in other ways, however, they are sharply contrasted areas, not least with respect to religious life.

It would be a great mistake to underestimate such differences.[14]

Cutting across these regional variations are the contrasts between urban and rural life and a tendency for religion (traditionally observed) to persist more strongly in rural communities; a tendency that may be equally true for common religion. Indeed David Clark's admirable portrait of common religion in the North Yorkshire fishing village of Staithes concludes by asking how far his analysis can be applied more generally in contemporary society. Is religion – both conventional but more especially common – dependent on the strength of the local community?

> The evidence from Staithes suggests that folk religion and the local community are interrelated phenomena. What can the analysis tell us about the nature of religion in the wider context? Do similar folk elements persist among those who live in the towns and industrial conurbations of a highly segmented and associational society?[15]

Important questions follow from this. Should we, for example, regard our large industrial conurbations as areas of uniform hopelessness, where religious practice is low and where even common religion has a more tenuous existence? My own feeling is that this rather negative conclusion implies certain assumptions, not all of which may be justified. For instance, are modern cities completely devoid of communities anyway;[16] do 'diluted' communities imply 'diluted' folk elements; or is common religion such a persistent force that it will find an alternative means of supporting itself within a city context? All these are possible answers to Clark's questions, each of them needs to be checked from an empirical point of view – and on the whole the work here still remains to be done. We cannot just assume that common religion is essentially a rural feature because it is more easily recognisable in a small community such as Staithes.

Moreover, even within one city different localities will vary very considerably from a religious point of view. Again we can take Liverpool as an example.[17] Within this diverse city there are areas which are still predominantly sectarian in their outlook; this certainly provides the dominant theme in their religious thinking.[18] Other parts of the city are much more concerned with ethnic problems and a multicultural aspect to society. Newer communities such as Kirkby or Speke do not have religious (or any other) traditions; their thinking will be different again. And in contrast there are – presumably – still a few longstanding working-class areas, untouched by planners and clearance schemes, where patterns may have existed for some generations. Religious life in Liverpool is by no means uniform, and very local dimensions may have a considerable influence on the way an individual looks at his life in relation to the church and to religious ideas; indeed these may well outweigh social or economic factors.[19]

If this were not complicated enough, further 'layers' emerge if we press the distinction between religious beliefs in the abstract and attitudes towards the church, though how far such distinctions are maintained by individuals is a difficult question. Put the other way round, how far do 'bad' experiences with the local church colour views about the church in a wider perspective and, perhaps more fundamentally, how far do they impinge on our beliefs about God? What does the word 'church' convey anyway – a building, a personality, a group of people, a national institution, the Royal Wedding or the international Pope? Are any of these ideas related to each other? What influence does the local church's policy on baptism have? How significant are denominational differences or questions of churchmanship? What are the consequences of closing a familiar building, of changes in liturgy, of particular clerical appointments? All these (and more) aspects interact with the more sociological questions outlined above and with the ups and downs of an individual's life.

Living in an area designated as deprived is only one of an almost infinite number of variables in these rather complicated equations. Furthermore, remembering that common religion is essentially thematic and not systematic, it is not necessarily the case that the selection of religious attitudes for any one person is internally consistent; indeed the reverse is much more likely to be the case.[20] We have come a long way from the universal emphasis of Greeley's thesis.

Is it possible then – with the help of sociological thinking – to see any themes or patterns that emerge in this confused area? One way of answering this question is to look at the various approaches that sociologists themselves have made to the subject and to review very briefly some of their methods and conclusions. Indeed, one of these approaches is that which has been implied right through this chapter, that is the stress on relating religious beliefs to a particular social context – a way of thinking taken from the sociology of knowledge. The result of applying this kind of theory is, however, to realise just how complicated the context is when looked at more closely. It heightens our awareness but points away from simple explanations.

In conclusion, I would like briefly to consider one or two other approaches that may shed some light on this subject, though it is clear that no single theory is in any way adequate by itself. Moreover, these approaches relate to a series of questions that we mentioned earlier; that is, how religious beliefs are acquired in the first place, how they are transmitted and how they are articulated – themes that are closely related to each other. A final note will consider attitudes towards organisations in general (not only religious ones) and how such attitudes vary within our society.

For some commentators, early childhood experiences are the key to understanding society;[21] patterns of socialisation therefore become of paramount importance in their analysis of contemporary life. Whilst having reservations about this approach as an all-encompassing theory, I feel that it is certainly helpful in understanding patterns of religiosity. Religion – like language (we will come back to the relationship between these) – is, largely, acquired rather than learnt, and much of this acquisition takes place within the family at a very early age.[22] Religious notions are, therefore, strongly related to a particular cultural inheritance and they are absorbed as part of a whole package of wisdom, some worldly, some otherworldly. And since these packages vary across society in important though very subtle ways, it seems likely that their religious aspects will vary with them. Obviously any over-rigid imposition of this kind of theory is distorting – our culture is not divided into isolated units, each with its own internally consistent thought world – but the general approach may help us to draw out certain emphases which will clarify our thinking on this subject.

For example, religious views acquired in this way are largely unexamined assumptions; they exist as almost unconscious parts of an individual's thinking. They are not necessarily static but tend to remain in a fairly latent form until 'needed'. What triggers the need varies, but it is often the major crises of life that bring religious ideas to the fore and such crises may even alter some of the original assumptions embodied in those ideas. Whether or not this is the case depends to some extent on the particular way in which the crisis is resolved, and important in this is the part that conventional religion (and its institutional representative) plays. Do the semiconscious themes and conventional teaching fit together or not? Which one is likely to predominate? Are traditional views reinforced or shaken? Do people move closer to the institutional church or feel more estranged from it? Each encounter of this kind may well be different, but one important factor in this interaction is both the width and the nature of the gap between the two aspects of religion, that is between conventional teaching and everyday beliefs.

Such gaps depend on a wide variety of factors, but one of

these is undoubtedly the ability to express oneself verbally (or the lack of such ability) and in addition the manner in which such verbalisation takes place. Indeed, a whole thread that underlies a study of this kind is the profoundly inarticulate nature of common religion and the need to be aware of this.[23] For this reason I feel that exploration of this whole area – possibly making use of Bernstein's language theories and developing their application to religious life – could prove (indeed has proved in limited instances) a very fruitful line of research. It will certainly highlight the gulf between conventional religious language and that of a very large sector of the population. And remembering that religious views are to a large extent picked up in the same way that language is, the two aspects of the problem are likely to be closely related.[24]

It is difficult to mention Bernstein's language theories without getting swept into educational issues and educational sociology, and the parallels between some of these and religious questions will be an approach taken up again in the next chapter. In the meantime it is important just to note that sociologists are right to emphasise the role of schools in the teaching of religion, and to stress that, despite everything, this still remains an important area of religious socialisation.[25] Moreover, the manner in which religious education is attempted is an important factor in how children come to view religion; all kinds of assumptions are involved which may or may not fit with existing views – either those absorbed at home or those suggested by institutional religion. The degree to which any of these strands overlap or, conversely, the lack of similarity between them (that is between home, school and church) will certainly have its effect on an individual's thinking.[26]

Acquisition, transmission and articulation of belief become, therefore, different facets of one problem; and through the differences in these processes, we begin to see variations in the nature of belief across society. Moreover, the importance of relating religiosity to other aspects of a subculture becomes even clearer. A final note regarding the attitude of many working-class people to organisations in general will provide a further illustration of this point.

If religious institutions feel that they struggle in certain areas of our society, it is undoubtedly true that they share in this the experience of many other organisations. The problem seems to stem from a certain hostility to authority, whether political, educational, religious or whatever. However, the degree to which the church is seen as being part of this alien world – that is, another 'them' to be mistrusted or, as far as possible, held at arm's length – depends a very great deal on the church's local representatives and their ability to disarm suspicions; personalities quite definitely count for a great deal.[27] However, even the very best of these individuals inevitably encounter some aspects of the problem, for the church is indeed an institution and as such is committed to its own maintenance.[28] This aim, whether it is realised or not, may well conflict with other goals; among these is the finding of an appropriate form of ministry in certain kinds of communities. At the moment, however, we can draw from this line of enquiry the fact that a generally high level of belief, together with a relative friendliness to at least some of the church's personnel as individuals, is not necessarily contradicted by a reluctance to attend, let alone participate actively in, an organisation; in parts of our society this is entirely 'normal'. Conversely a lack of religious activity need not necessarily imply a lack of religious belief *per se*, though it might well have consequences for the nature of that belief.

Indeed it is clear that among working-class people in particular, churchgoing is plainly not seen as a necessary part of Christianity. Rather, according to the Leeds survey, the stress falls more or less equally on belief in God and leading a good life;[29] regular church attendance is often rather bluntly categorised as hypocrisy. This divorce of sentiment from churchgoing seems to be the crucial element in our understanding, for if belief is separated from active participation it is then far more susceptible to other currents of thought, both religious and non-religious;[30] these currents in fact form one aspect of the local context for believing. The importance of such subcultures and their influence on different aspects of religiosity is the principal theme underlying each of the theoretical approaches outlined above (all of which could be developed at some length). In the final chapter, this point will be taken further as we look at the peculiar relationship between conventional and common religion, stressing the possible variations in the relationship in different parts of our society.

4

THE RELATIONSHIP BETWEEN CONVENTIONAL AND COMMON RELIGION

An important preliminary to discussing these two aspects of religiosity is the need to realise that any distinction between them is an academic perception not on the whole shared by the participant. Moreover, almost everyone's religious views contain elements of both conventional orthodoxy and common religion; only a rarefied few, if any, will avoid the latter altogether. On the whole churchgoers are more 'orthodox' than non-churchgoers, but common religion certainly intrudes beyond the church door to some extent at least.

With this in mind we can go back to an earlier section and pick up the point that not all parts of the particular religious package that we evolve for ourselves will necessarily be compatible with orthodox Christian theology. Indeed, what arises in practice derives from the cumulative effect of a large number of individual choices, most of which incorporate blurred distinctions and a somewhat approximate grasp of Christian doctrine. In this process each of us draws from whatever is 'available' and selects (often passively) what is most appropriate or meaningful for us. There is little that is black or white in these matters, and almost every conceivable shade of grey.

Of considerable (and unavoidable) importance in this

grey area are the 'Christian' aspects of common religion, expressed in the tendency to approach the churches at certain times in life to mark a particular event with an appropriate ceremony. The Church of England has a larger constituency in this respect than the other English churches and is therefore under more pressure to evolve an appropriate policy from a pastoral point of view. It is immediately apparent, however, that reactions to this pressure vary a very great deal even within Anglicanism. Some churches, for example, accept such approaches without any precondition, arguing that folk religion (this is the term generally used in this context) is something that the local church can build on; it provides a channel that must be kept open at all costs. Other parishes are less happy about this policy, feeling more strongly about doctrinal matters and arguing that the church should be very careful in its definition of membership.

Both points of view are to some extent justified. A strong strand of common religion may indeed bring requests for baptism, church marriage and Christian burial, through which valuable contact may be made; this is undeniable. At the same time, however, this very strength may be a challenge to the church in that common religion comes to provide an adequate alternative to conventional Christianity and the more adequate the alternative, the less need the individual will have to seek explanations for life's problems within the orthodox teaching of the church. Common religion emerges as a rival rather than a source of recruitment. Indeed, it is sometimes argued that the 'acceptors' are in fact encouraging their rival rather than building up the church.

To others this seems unnecessarily negative, and in practice most churches evolve a system that lies somewhere between the two extremes. It is, however, important to grasp that these are indeed complex issues where particular policies may have unexpected results. Moreover, merely reversing the policy does not always solve the problem; it may serve only to create a new set of difficulties. For example, in the case of refusing baptism, rejection and bitterness can be a very high price – perhaps too high – to pay for doctrinal purity.

From a sociological point of view, however, this controversial issue has a further dimension. Underlying the whole question is the very ambivalent nature of the relationship between conventional and common religion, and it is this point that I would like to stress in particular. Inextricably linked, the two are not necessarily in conflict, but neither are they totally in harmony. Sociologically, it seems that one tends to fill the gaps left by the other, and so to some extent at least each disguises the deficiencies of the other.[1] From the point of view of church policy, the situation is more problematic; this is hardly surprising, bearing in mind the intricate relationship between the two aspects of religion.[2]

Complex though this question is, it is essential that the churches try to understand it. For, as the various surveys outlined in the introduction have shown, the numbers claiming some sort of religious belief in our society stay fairly constant (including the figures for the 1980s), despite the fact that religious attendance has fallen very considerably in recent decades. The results would seem to be an increasing number of people susceptible to the ideas of common religion without the direction that comes from more or less regular contact with at least some orthodox teaching.[3] Indeed it could be argued that this drifting of 'belief' away from mainline Christian teaching is in fact a greater challenge to the contemporary church than the supposedly secular nature of the society in which we live.

If this relationship between conventional and common religion is one that we cannot avoid, does it have particular stresses or strains depending on the kind of parish involved? For example, and again going back to a point raised earlier, certain sections of our society – while being just as likely on an individual level to hold religious views that conflict with orthodox theology – are at least nearer to the church in other respects, in their manner of speech and in their acceptance of organisations *per se* without hostility. In consequence, it is possible that for them the 'gap' between the two aspects of religion may be more easily bridged. On the other hand, this very similarity may in itself cause a problem: the distinctions are more likely to be blurred, and what is acceptable culturally (because expressed appropriately) becomes acceptable theologically – middle-classness begins to merge into Christianity. These are two sides of one question which are not easily disentangled.

In contrast, the cultural gap in some working-class areas of society is a problem to which we have already referred. In these parts of society churchgoing never was a regular habit and the few who attended are now even fewer; in consequence the potential for unorthodox belief is probably higher. Moreover, the language contrast is more pronounced and the institutional aspect of the church arouses more hostility. It seems, though, that religious belief (to a considerable extent at least) maintains itself. If we follow the same sort of pattern as before, it may be more difficult – probably much more – for the church to attain any sort of conventional success; large attendances are, and for the foreseeable future always will be, most unlikely. On the other hand, the blurring of distinctions is going to be equally rare; a fact that could perhaps be a positive advantage to the church. The latter point is debatable, and in itself is probably of little encouragement to those whose churches are never filled and who struggle in consequence with feelings of failure.

Should these full churches, however, necessarily be the principal criterion of success? It seems to me that a minister who is sensitive to the subculture in which he works may begin to think otherwise, and the church should be prepared to give him support in a different type of ministry. It may be that the nature of belief in parts of our urban society is indeed one aspect of the church's difficulties in such areas, but only if its ministry is assessed in particular terms. If it is true that some gaps may be too large to bridge, others may appear less formidable if looked at from a different perspective.

For example, to invite a certain kind of person to a service and hand them an *Alternative Service Book* of more than a thousand pages when reading doesn't come easily is likely to increase the gap.[4] To provide practical support and help with writing a letter (together with the confidence to ask for such help in the first place) for that same individual is likely to reduce it. Both gestures are equally valid forms of ministry and both involve the ability to articulate; in the first case this is used negatively, in the second it is used positively. Indeed, careful and sensitive use of this particular gift can transform a situation and provide a way forward which avoids two alternative dangers; that is, either to underestimate the difficulties that some congregations have in this respect or, conversely, to try overhard to minimise differences between clergy and people in certain types of parish.[5]

Sensitive ministry has, however, a much wider application. If the church's aim might be described as the need to create contexts in which 'belief' can emerge from a semiconscious level and be gradually transformed into something closer to an authentic Christian faith,[6] it does not follow that this aim is always achieved in a uniform way. What is appropriate for one part of society is less appropriate for another. If, for example, there is a willingness to attend church in the area, this can provide a starting point on which to build; if this is not the case, then other methods may be equally valid. The tendency of the church to equate only the former with success is a one-sided assessment of the situation. Indeed, persisting along such lines in parts of our society may only serve to alienate, to reinforce divisions, rather than to heal rifts. Obviously such emphases (to work, as it were, within or without the church) are two aspects of ministry which are not necessarily mutually exclusive. It seems likely, however, that they will, or should, exist in different proportions in different kinds of parish.[7]

Bearing this in mind, and without becoming too involved in educational matters, it may be helpful to see the parallels that face those responsible for educational policy. It is manifest that in certain parts of society educational achievement remains worryingly low if measured by the conventional means of success in examinations – the system appears to have failed. Moreover, attempts to restructure this aspect of education and make it more appropriate to the needs of certain communities inevitably bring howls of dismay from those whose children do well and who need the qualifications obtained by means of exams. Balancing the two different needs, and all those between them, becomes increasingly difficult within a system whose workforce is already hard pressed and whose finance is barely adequate. The ideal of variety is not, however, disputed.

Moreover, on a more individual level I have been struck by a further possible parallel between church structures and educational ones. While having every sympathy for those in Liverpool who have pioneered the parent governor movement,[8] it does not surprise me that in parts of the city it has at times been difficult to persuade people to fulfil this role. Even the kindest and most sympathetic chairman or headmaster (and this can by no means be taken for granted) will have to work hard to overcome the formality inherent in the committee structure. Encouraging an individual to take part in this process perhaps has a counterpart in inviting someone to take part in a parochial church council meeting; each of these committees involves formal agendas, long-term planning and a certain manner of doing business. Both can seem hostile to those unused to such procedures.

A further point follows from this. A lack of participation

in these formal structures (both educational and ecclesiastical) is often wrongly interpreted. It does not imply the
absence of constructive ideas, still less of strong feelings.
Indeed closing a local school can provoke much the same
sort of reaction as closing a church: often an unexpected
vehemence along the lines of 'why us?', 'why our school?',
and sometimes some very direct action indeed. It does,
however, indicate a certain hesitation about expressing
ideas or opinions in a particular – rather alien – way.[9]

However, in one very important respect, the church as
an institution differs from other organisations committed
to working in areas of deprivation. Whereas a very large
majority of teachers, social workers, health workers, doc-
tors, and even politicians return to the suburbs at the end
of the working day, this is not true of the clergyman, who
lives – as it were – above the shop. Of course this increases
the strain borne by him and his family, since he will often be
the first port of call for those who need his help – simply by
availability out of office hours; on the other hand, he will be
in a better place than most to know fairly precisely what is
going on in the area. A sensitive man, well supported by
the wider church, can play a very strategic role in our
increasingly polarised society. Aware of the subculture in
which he ministers, he can provide a bridge between this
and other parts of society – a bridge that encourages
communications in both directions. This role, however,
will not be possible if the minister is beset by doubts about
failure because the church remains empty on Sundays, if he
is left to manage entirely alone and if his family are not
given the support they, as well as he, deserve.

In stressing this commitment to remain physically
present in the inner city, I am reminded of a passage in
Frankenberg's book on communities.[10] In this, the young
anthropologist sits rather dejectedly on a hill overlooking
the village that he wants to study, unable to find a way into
it. Only in participating, in committing himself to local
activities, can he gain a foothold and begin his work.

Within the context of the inner city, the church has already got this foothold and needs not only to keep it but to build on it. To withdraw because the going is tough will widen the gap between that particular subculture and the institutional church – a gesture that is unlikely to further an effective ministry. Moreover, in remaining present the church is not only furthering its own aims, it is fulfilling an increasingly important function for society. The parochial structure may show signs of strain in certain parts of our cities; it is, however, a vital link with a way of life that is in danger of being increasingly misunderstood by many people.[11]

If we attempt now to draw some of these ideas together, it is clear that the nature of belief does indeed vary within our society; the third chapter attempted to show the very many factors that may be involved in these variations, economic deprivation being only one of them. Furthermore, the very real and cumulative nature of the problems of urban priority areas makes life in these areas difficult for everyone who has to share them, including those who work there on behalf of the various churches. In no way should this fact be underestimated.[12]

However, to concentrate on the nature of belief in parts of our cities and to ask whether this in itself constitutes a particular difficulty for ministry is a separate question. In some ways the task is more demanding in that the cultural gap between the institutional church and everyday beliefs is likely to be a wide one. Moreover, from a historical point of view the church has done 'better' in some areas than others; a fact which in itself has consequences for the nature of belief in that parts of our society have been without close contact with the church for several generations. On the other hand, in persisting with this definition of 'better', it seems that the church itself may exacerbate the problem. In particular, it is asking for success measured in terms that are not as appropriate in the inner city as they are in the suburbs. Large congregations are going to be the exception rather than the rule, for regular attendance or organisational commitment are unlikely.[13] An individual priest – particularly one who is well attuned to the needs of his people – may, however, be able to find alternative and effective ways of ministering to them in order to draw out their belief and to nurture this closer to the Christian faith. A flexible approach to his role and a more reasonable expectation of what is possible may well release an individual's potential; this seems more sensible than always trying to channel his energies in ways that are not very likely to bear fruit.

In its implication for the church's ministry, the nature of belief within society does not so much vary along an easy-hard continuum, rather its variations require in practice particular sensitivities and gifts which will not always be the same; effective ministry is never 'easy'. It seems, however, that the church has tended to train its clergy to think in terms which may be more appropriate for one kind of ministry than another. Moreover, if expectations are not fulfilled it may be difficult to avoid feelings of failure and a loss of morale. Alongside this, it is clear that the organisational aspects of the church have inclined it towards some social groups rather than others. Perhaps it is these implicit assumptions within the church, in addition to – or indeed, rather more than – the nature of belief outside it, that make the task of the church within areas of urban deprivation seem so daunting.

Appendix A

CONVENTIONAL RELIGION AND COMMON RELIGION IN LEEDS

The genesis and development of the research project based at the sociology department in Leeds and directed by Dr Robert Towler are well documented in the series of research papers published as part of the project itself. These are listed below.

To some extent the project has proved a controversial one in that relatively little new material has emerged from it up to now, though a further book based on the project is anticipated.[1] On the other hand, it has undoubtedly provided a large body of empirical material on religious belief and the variables associated with this. This material derives from the survey (in the autumn of 1982) of some 1,600 Leeds people, each of whom answered a lengthy questionnaire covering a wide variety of common religion themes. The computerised results are held at present in Leeds, but there is in addition a permanent copy of this data at the Economic and Social Research Council Archive at the University of Essex. As the result of a survey, this material is bound to be subject to the criticisms levelled at this type of approach to religious information. On the other hand, of its kind, the survey instrument used in this case was exceptionally well prepared and the potential within the material collected could still be high if funds would permit further research.[2] At the moment, however, funds are exhausted and most of the personnel involved in the study have moved away from Leeds.

Moreover, from the point of view of further work on the nature of belief in urban priority areas, Dr Towler felt that the Leeds material would not be that much use directly; the cell sizes in the Leeds inner-city areas would be small and there would be no way of knowing whether the households interviewed there were in any way typical of the area. On the other hand, the Leeds sample is on the whole felt to be a highly representative one, and their results could be used as a comparative base against which inner-city material could be evaluated.

In a more indirect way, the background work to the Leeds study, the careful use of terms and the surveys of related literature have been of considerable use in preparing this material. In addition, I am most grateful to Dr Kim Knott and Helen Krarup at Leeds, who took much time and trouble to discuss this subject with me as did Dr Towler himself. I have drawn considerably on the various research papers published by the project, in particular for bibliographic information, for discussions of methodological problems and for insight into the role of the media with relation to both conventional and common religion. Other more specific points are alluded to in the footnotes.

The University of Leeds, Department of Sociology, Religious Research Papers

1 Final Report on HR6914.
2 Research Grant Application: Conventional religion and common religion in Leeds.
3 Methodological Problems in the Study of Implicit Religion.
4 Hinduism in England: The Hindu Population in Leeds.
5 A Preliminary Document on 'Media Portrayals

of Religion and their Reception: A Leeds-based Study'.

6   Muslims, Sikhs and Hindus in the UK: problems in the estimation of religious statistics.

7   End of year report 1980–1981: Conventional religion and common religion in Leeds (HR7720).

8   A guide to the computer-based bibliographic facilities of the project 'Conventional religion and common religion in Leeds'.

9   'Conventional and common religion in the media', the transcript of a talk given at the IBA Religious Broadcasting Consultation, April 1983.

10 End of year report January 1982–January 1983: Conventional religion and common religion in Leeds (HR7720).

11 Conventional religion and common religion in Great Britain.

12 'Conventional religion and common religion in Leeds', Interview Schedule: Basic frequencies by question.

Appendix B

THE NETWORK FOR THE STUDY OF IMPLICIT RELIGION

The Network for the Study of Implicit Religion was initiated in the late 1970s by Canon Dr Edward Bailey, who now regularly contacts over a thousand individuals (not all in Britain) and provides through a variety of conferences an extensive forum for debate in the field of implicit religion. These conferences vary in nature from the academic to those held for clergy or ordinands, including those that relate in particular to religious education and the role of implicit religion in this rather specific field.[1]

In addition to creating this forum for discussion, Dr Bailey holds a collection of documents available to enquirers and publishes a considerable amount on this subject.[2] His own work is based for the most part on the notion that implicit religion is concerned 'with the religious implications of everyday life . . . By this is meant, not the implications of everyday life for (say) the Christian religion, but the consideration of ordinary life as itself containing implications that may have a religious character.'[3] The definition, therefore, is a wider one than that outlined by Towler and his associates, but it does have the useful emphasis of seeing differences with respect to beliefs, whether implicit or explicit, between different sectors of society. Each group or community may have a different integrating focus.[4] This aspect of Bailey's work I have retained while concentrating primarily on the common religion definition deriving from the Leeds study; I have felt the latter to be a more useful approach, bearing in mind the particular questions put to me by the Archbishop's Commission.[5]

A final point that I discussed at some length with Dr Bailey was the notion that the role of the churches or of church people should be to create conditions or contexts in which the unexpressed or inarticulate 'spirit' can surface. Curiously, exactly the same idea was suggested by Margaret Simey in relation to her experience as a councillor in Toxteth. That a certain spiritual pool existed even in an area torn by devastation was not questioned; in Lady Simey's view the church existed to draw this out, to bring to the surface what for the most part lies buried so deep that many observers overlook it altogether. This religion below street-level is perhaps another way of describing David Martin's subterranean theologies – that 'luxuriant theological undergrowth which provides the working core of belief more often than is realised'.[6] That such a core of belief should continue to exist at all in areas of such acute deprivation is in itself a tribute to its strength and persistence.

Appendix C

BELIEVING AND BELONGING

It is quite clear that a very large number of people in this country say that they believe in God but do not belong to a church as normally conceived. On the other hand, precisely these individuals when asked for information about church membership on an official form of one kind or another will respond positively rather than negatively and would not be pleased if this membership was challenged. What then do these terms mean; should affiliation, for example, be separated from membership?[1]

Conversely, there are other parts of our society where membership of a particular religious group is perhaps of more importance than the associated belief. In the last century this was certainly true for Irish immigrants, whose Irish identity became associated with Roman Catholicism and for whom church membership expressed something considerably more than a particular version of Christian theology. Moreover, it seems likely that the same process is occurring among more recent immigrants to this country. Whether these are relatively small groups – for example, the Greek population who centre their activities on the local Greek Orthodox church – or much larger ethnic minorities – for example, West Indians who find not only an opportunity to express their belief but also a much needed sense of identity in black-led Pentecostal churches – it is quite clear that the relationship between believing and belonging is for them very different from what this implies for the nominal English-born Anglican.

Once again, the historical context in which belief or belonging takes place provides one clue to understanding their relationship; for example, a minority church will always be different from a majority one in this respect. If the Roman Catholic Church in this country maintains a relatively high membership among working people, even within large conurbations, this is not true of the Roman Church in France or Italy. This relative success within the British context is not a result of Catholicism *per se*, but rather one consequence of a minority wanting to retain a certain identity. Moreover, the association between Catholicism and Irishness gives at least part of the Catholic minority in this country its rather specific flavour; a point that cannot be understood without a knowledge of the relevant history.[2]

Similarly, the fact that most ethnic groups and their associated churches are bound to see themselves to some extent as minorities whose identity is threatened will encourage certain aspects of their church life rather than others. Membership, or at least a strong sense of affiliation, will be important, for often it is through religious organisations that other aspects of the culture are kept alive. Appreciating this point may go some way to correct the distortions that result from categorising individuals inappropriately. For example, listing South Asians as Indians, Pakistanis or Bangladeshis tells us their country of origin but disguises their religious and to some extent their ethnic identity. 'Hindu', 'Sikh' and 'Muslim' are of greater use in studying identity, though each of these categories may well represent more than one ethnic enclave and gloss over what are the effective community boundaries.[3]

Alongside these historical pressures, however, theological influences do also play a part in determining how far belief is likely to synchronise with belonging. As a broad example of this, one can contrast the Baptist community with Anglicanism. For the Baptists, full membership associated with believers' baptism is conditional upon a public statement of belief. In consequence, those who claim membership in this particular church form a close-knit, theologically well-defined community. In contrast, the inclusive nature of the Anglican church, blurred at the edges almost by definition, with relatively little insistence on doctrinal commitment, is bound to result in a very different sort of community. Clearly we cannot ignore theological pressures when considering the relationship between believing and belonging, though in practice it is not always easy to disentangle purely theological pressures from their social context.[4]

Moreover, if the contrast between the Baptists and Anglicanism demonstrates this as an overall pattern, there are – as we have seen – a number of significant variations within Anglicanism. Certain congregations within the Church of England insist to a greater degree than others on doctrinal matters, and their attitude to membership will vary accordingly. A willingness or not to baptise the children of non-churchgoers is one result of such influences, but in addition the whole nature of the community surrounding a congregation of a theologically 'pure' type will be different from that surrounding a church with a different kind of theological commitment.

Cutting across these theological differences, however, are the social and cultural contexts in which these churches minister. It is clear that some of these contexts are more favourable than others to churchgoing as a pattern of social life. In consequence – to take two extremes – it will be easier, or at least much more 'normal', for a family (in particular a mother and children) or a single lady to attend a church in a middle-class suburb than for a working-class man in other parts of the same city. It may be, therefore, that membership – in the form of attendance – in the suburb means something different from membership in the inner city, for churchgoing in the suburb fits much better with the existing pattern of life and so may 'demand' less, at least in the first instance. Moreover, this difference can be seen between Anglican churches that from the point of view of theology are rather similar in type; the two variables have to be considered together.[5]

Indeed, if believing and belonging are themselves considered as two variables, each of which lies along a different continuum and each of which is subject to a whole range of influences – historical (for example, a majority or a minority church), theological, national and local, cultural and subcultural (all of which, furthermore, interact on each other) – we can begin to appreciate the complexity of the situation. The point of intersection between the two variables will be determined by a whole variety of factors, not all of which will necessarily operate in the same direction. Add to these factors, as before, influences such as the personality of the minister, peculiarly local problems with buildings, personal likes and dislikes regarding liturgy, individual or family crises, and it becomes difficult to predict with any certainty how the two factors will interrelate. Certain combinations may be more likely than others, but the range of possibilities remains a wide one.

Part Two

**'I do believe in Christmas'
White working-class people and Anglican
clergy in inner-city London**

by

Geoffrey Ahern

Research commissioned by the Christian Evidence
Society

ACKNOWLEDGMENTS

This research developed from the inspiration of the Rev. Dr Julian Scharf; and funding from the Christian Evidence Society made it possible.

I will not single out most of the Tower Hamlets clergy who contributed so freely of their time and counsel, since the second part of this paper consists of an account of meetings with them. However, I may mention the assistance of others, to whom I am no less grateful: the Rev. Dr Edward Bailey, Alan Bartlett, Dr Melanie Cottrell, Dr Grace Davie, the Rev. Richard Harries, the Rev. David Hewitt, the Rev. Jeremy Hutchinson, the Rev. Professor David Martin, Dr Hugh McLeod, the Rev. John Pearce, John Pearson, Dr Robert Towler, Dr Andrew Walker, David Wasdell and Dr Bryan Wilson. The responsibility for the design, execution and presentation of this research has been mine alone.

Geoffrey Ahern

'If you ain't got nothing nobody won't come to give you anything' – from Tower Hamlets, 1985.

'My position is productive of what I might venture to call mental torture' – Victor of St Andrews, Bethnal Green, 1858.[1]

5

PROLOGUE: REFLECTIONS ON FIELDWORK AND THE NATURE OF BELIEF

This part of the book describes fieldwork which was carried out recently in inner-city London. In its report stage it was entitled 'Cockneys and Clergy Speak. A sectarian Anglicanism for the inner-city?'

Many readers will be all too familiar with the inner city, living in it, or working with it as a constant background. Fieldwork provides a different kind of knowledge: it is a preplanned encounter in which, for a relatively short period of time, other people's everyday background is singled out, typically by someone who does not belong, as a focus for study. How this encounter is engineered drastically affects the content of what will be found out. Hence the methods of research are very important. In the account that follows they are described first of all. This tight entrance is provided for those readers whose interest in this research goes beyond the impressionistic.

The fieldwork was with people drawn from two groups, the white working class and the Anglican clergy. Much more is written on the former than on 'them people' (as the latter were once described). My attempt has been to present the values and ways of life of others, and so to restrict the interference of comment to a minimum, in the middle chapters. This approach will be familiar to readers who are aware of research methods in anthropology and the social sciences.

There is an abrupt change in the final chapter, which, with its heading 'Recommendations', starts rashly and continues in the same vein. Because those who commissioned this research did so out of a sense of pastoral urgency, the scholarly purity of the research role is left behind. This was the most difficult chapter to construct, and I am painfully aware of the likely limitations of any actions that can be taken in the inner city by religious agencies, especially those (like the Church of England) that are, or are taken to be, representative of authority.

Many might assume that the most deprived areas in our society will be the most atheist in belief, even though there is considerable evidence to suggest that in the UK as a whole – and elsewhere – the decline in institutional religion has not been accompanied by a proportionate take-over by rational humanism. Instead, people's views seem to be as full of unchristian metaphysics, as self-contradictory and, at the level of the individual, as unpredictable as they probably always have been in this country.

My explorations in carefully preselected areas of London's working-class Tower Hamlets did not turn up much in the way of out-and-out atheism. In middle-class Highgate, Hampstead, and the more prettified parts of Islington, London may indeed be more explicitly disbelieving.

Indeed, the very structure of 'belief', or of its mirror-image 'disbelief', is probably most pronounced among the educated, or the self-aware classes. 'He believes in the life-force', 'She believes in love', 'John is a materialist' (the word 'believe' may be left out): the truth of much middle-class personal identity is negotiated through the discrimination of differing beliefs. In Tower Hamlets, in contrast, I sensed that personal identity is much less dependent on abstractions for its definition. 'Belief' itself would seem to be one of the privileges that has left the concrete world of white working-class Tower Hamlets by.

If we need to think that everyone 'has to believe in something', the wool may be being pulled over our eyes by our own cultural conditioning. Of the three great monotheistic religions, Judaism, Christianity and Islam, it is Christianity that has most defined itself through creed; unlike Judaism, it has not made its priority the following of accumulated wisdom, prescribed by experts, of a 'divinely' selected ethnic group, and, unlike Islam, its main emphasis is not on submission. Protestant Christianity (and its secular offshoot, scientistic atheism) defines itself more by the credo than does its Catholic matrix. In the Hindu way of life, *dharma*, an untranslatable idea linking inner state, caste-duty and cosmos, predominates; for the practising Buddhist, unless he follows one of the varieties that have all but reversed the recorded teachings of the founder, belief seems to be seen by some stage along the path as nothing but an impermanent and delusory compound of self and world. In contrast, the Western intellectual, especially the priest, but also the secular fieldworker, is likely to have been mentally structured into seeing the world in terms of 'belief' and 'disbelief'. It seems to me, particularly in longer-term retrospect, that belief in belief is a preconception of Western-influenced education. It is a mistake to project this mentality into the inner city.

My most lasting impression of white working-class Tower Hamlets – and I think it pervades the account that follows – is of the inappropriateness of the cultural concepts of 'belief' and 'disbelief'. For example, one of my respondents said, 'I do believe in Christmas.'

At first glance here it would appear that belief is alive and well. What could be more in the tradition of Protestant martyrs than 'I do believe'? But . . . belief in *Christmas*? The word 'believe' here seems to be used in an entirely different sense from belief in the life-force, from faith that Jesus was the Son of God, from an ideological package or secular abstraction. 'Believe' here relates to *social practice*; it has more in common with being a blood brother. The action in 'I do' is quite consistent with this. The potent objection to measuring belief in God through surveys – that it is impossible to know what people mean when they state that they do or do not believe in God – applies no less strongly to an uncritical application of the concept 'belief' to the inner city.

Both the clergy and other inhabitants of the inner city – and elsewhere – seem to suffer from the contemporary erosion of community. But the clergy, since they are generally at the abstract, liberal end of 'belief' culture, are very differently placed in their non-belonging from the atomised white working class in modern Tower Hamlets, and probably from most other inhabitants of today's inner city[2] (though these areas no doubt differ greatly as well, for example, as between Liverpool and London's East End). The social practice[3] most desired by the white working class in the latter seems generally to be ethnically particular and in contrast to the cultural relativism that underlies the radical social gospel. Forty-two interviews[4] have led me to suspect that those clergy who, in Tower Hamlets and similar areas, may most be able to accept the absence of a conventional middle-class 'belief' culture, may also be least able to accept the ethnically exclusive nature of the symbols that are most likely to bind the white working class in communal practice related to the sacred.

6

METHODS OF RESEARCH

There appears to have been no recent qualitative research
into the attitudes of white working-class non-churchgoers
towards the Church of England and Christian belief.[1]
Indigenous whites still seem to be the largest ethnic group
in Tower Hamlets. Thus understanding their outlook is not
only important in itself, it is also essential for placing the
problems of immigrant Bangladeshis, West Indians and
others in cultural context. Conversely, the contrast of
Islam and black Pentecostalism throws white working-class
culture into relief.

Twenty-four white working-class interviewees were recruited from two equal groups, the 'quota sample' and the
'baptism sample'. Both groups included only white working-class non-churchgoers who did not belong to non-
Anglican religious allegiances (for example, Catholicism,
Judaism).[2] None of the quota sample had agreed to have a
child baptised into the Church of England; the distin-
guishing criterion for the baptism sample was involvement
of some kind in the baptism of one or more children into
the Church of England.

Twelve Anglican clergy with whom meetings were also
held were each asked to name estates they deemed 'typical'
and relatively inhabited by the indigenous white working
class. This method was used partly so as not to include
estates that the clergy would not think of evangelising; as it
happened, the type of estate varied. From each of these

estates one person was singled out for interview by means of a quota method of selection.

The first six people interviewed, who would have been eligible for the quota sample, had they not been involved in the baptism of a child into the Church of England, comprised half the baptism sample. The other half were recruited from eleven parish lists (one interview per list used) of the white working-class non-churchgoers who had had a child most recently baptised. The twelve clergy were asked to provide these lists. The baptism sample were drawn from eleven out of the twelve areas represented by the clergy.[3]

The division into quota and baptism samples was made so that attitudinal differences could be assessed. Would the baptism sample's outlook suggest an inner band of more Anglican-minded people who compare with an outer band of indifference suggested by the quota sample? A diffusion and relative homogeneity of viewpoint was indicated by the mere process of putting this research design into operation. A very high proportion of people who agreed to be interviewed (perhaps 3 or 4:1) were not eligible for the quota sample because they had had a child baptised into the Church of England; also, many in the quota sample seemingly might have had a child baptised into the Church of England had circumstances other than their religious affiliations been different (for example, had they had a child, or had their spouse not been Catholic). Furthermore, many in the baptism sample had merely acquiesced in the baptism of their child. It would have been impracticable to refine the demarcation between the quota and baptism samples into greater meaningfulness, if only because it would then have become virtually impossible to fill up the quota.

The quota sample

Interrelated sex and age controls were used. A male and female each were interviewed from the following age-groups: 15–25; 25–35; 35–45; 45–55; 55–65; 65+ (i.e., twelve interviewees in all). The aim was to secure a rough spread of sex and age variables. People were found through going round the estates named by the clergy and making introductions on the doorstep.[4] Using contacts to secure personal introductions would have been easier, but would have introduced an unacceptable bias. The more random procedure adopted made it possible to have a wider range of interviewees and to form an impression of those who refused interviews.

The baptism sample

A control was applied so that overall there was a balance of the sexes. An even spread of ages was not secured, since it seemed desirable to recruit half the sample from lists of the most recent baptisms: thus it was a foregone conclusion that there would be an unavoidable skew towards the young middle aged.

At no stage was any connection with the Church of England, the clergy or baptismal lists stated or (I believe) implied to the six recruited from these lists. A standard letter was sent by way of introduction to 'the occupier' at the addresses on the lists, stating the research was 'into what Tower Hamlets people generally feel about the area in which they live and their opinions', and saying the letter might be followed up by a personal visit at weekends or in the evenings. Subsequent doorstep visits secured the interviews. The 'routine' information asked for included the subject's name; thus it was possible to check covertly on the doorstep that the name of the person agreeing to be interviewed corresponded with the surname(s) on the baptismal list.[5]

Self-selection

The refusal rate for the quota sample was especially high.[6] Contributory factors included the glut of research in Tower Hamlets (that this did not include the subject of this research could not be said) and the presence for several months past of a bogus doctor with a habit of assaulting children: on one occasion I was rushed at in the Vallance Road by two detectives and several constables because my self-description on someone's doorstep as a 'doctor of philosophy' had seemed close enough. The main reason for the high refusal rate probably was not that people doubted that I was who I said I was (I came with appropriate documentary identification); it was probably that patently I was much what I said I was. My self-introduction did not mention religion; but I could not avoid saying I was a researcher doing university-type research[7] for the C. S. Lewis Centre. (The latter had to be included if I was asked – as I usually was – but I assumed that no one had heard of C. S. Lewis in a way that connected him with Christianity.) I did not belong and was some kind of snooper.

The bias resulting from this self-selection was probably considerable. Those interviewed were almost entirely 'Cockneys' – those born and bred in the East End – with very few people who had moved in from outside (despite the fact that clergy said that the GLC had housed very many white working-class problem families from London generally in Tower Hamlets). The cultural attributes of a sociologist of religion, like those of an Anglican clergyman, will probably be least rejected by the 'upper' working class. That this is the major, unavoidable, blind spot of this research is suggested by the fact that class was little mentioned as such by the interviewees. The diffusion and relative homogeneity of viewpoint between the quota and baptism samples mentioned earlier in this paper needs to be interpreted in the light of what seems to have been a disproportionately high refusal rate on the part of the most rootless and mobile working class.

A direct warmth of heart generally lay behind those doors that were opened. I felt I learnt, as I went round the estates, that what worked best in getting access (even more than elsewhere) was a bearing that was expressive, open and not too serious.[8] The many hours spent on the doorstep were very informative and have contributed towards the interpretation of the harder information collected.

Interviews as a method for assessing values and beliefs

Interviews can ensure that key issues are covered within a relatively short time, also they can be relatively representatively targeted, compared to 'anthropological' methods of information gathering. The great disadvantage of interviews, even when (as here) as unstructured as possible, is that they tend to be a forcing technique that produces unrealistically cut and dried answers. The overall context of the interview – even though called a 'meeting' – carries its own expectations. The danger here is that Tower Hamlets opinion will be distorted in an intellectualist way.

The alternative method of participant observation was an option. It was rejected because it would yield that little knowledge that is a dangerous thing (because much less directed than almost any interview could be). Total immersion in the culture for a year would be a very different – and very much more resource-consuming – matter. In my opinion, this is the only technique that can validly 'get at' the nebulous area of 'implicit religion' in a qualitative way.[9] Here interviews were used to uncover the more straightforwardly commissioned subject: attitudes towards the Church of England and Christianity. This is the question of most immediate concern to Anglican clergy in Tower Hamlets.

The interviews

These were all tape-recorded[10] with, generally, no trouble (in what seems to be an electronically-minded culture). Often others were around – particularly husbands, where wives were the subjects – so the words of the interviewee, quite apart from my presence, sometimes arose out of a dyadic or even triadic process. Such combinations seemed unavoidable (however, I always managed to get the front room television switched off). In negotiating interviews I usually specified twenty minutes, but the effective time probably averaged out as half an hour or longer.

After some discussion of estates, buildings, television and newspapers, it was almost always surprisingly easy to divert the interviewee's thoughts towards the subject matter of this research (generally through relating what was answered about reading the newspaper horoscope to what had been said about formal religious allegiance in the preliminary, 'routine' questions). Except in the case of the six interviews derived through baptismal lists, it generally seemed wise later to acknowledge that 'religion', the subject which has 'come up' (or something like this), had become salient to the research. At this stage I was sensing that the reactions were possibly becoming contaminated; I tried to avoid this (probably not always successfully) by saying I was only doing a job and did not mind what was said. This raising to consciousness also allowed interviewees to give more considered, balanced points of view. Thus for most of the interview there was a surreptitious approach;[11] this was generally followed towards the end, when most or all of the research subjects had been covered, by a conscious spotlight and a disclaimer of personal religious involvement or vulnerability.

7

'US', or BELONGING IN TOWER HAMLETS

This could well have been headed 'not belonging in Tower Hamlets'. Though about three-quarters of both the quota and baptism samples had apparently lived in Tower Hamlets all their lives, and only one of the twenty-four did not have roots in the area, there was considerable evidence of internal movement; only vestiges remained of the community and sense of localism that existed in Bethnal Green as late as the 1950s.[1] The imposition of 'Tower Hamlets' on to the East End is most visible in the estates themselves, since they do not vary according to vertical divisions of locality (Spitalfields, Bow, Shadwell, Mile End, Old Ford and other evocative names), but horizontally according to changes in the dictates of bureaucratic architectural fashion. The poverty-struck community in which doorsteps, which fronted real streets, were nevertheless scrubbed was probably doomed by heavy bombing in the war. The East End has shared something of the German experience of a *Jahr Null*, but subsequently has known no economic miracle.

The collective areas just about everywhere in the estates displayed the sub-animal degradation that appears when there are no social structures through which human order can assert itself: urine on the staircases, excrement everywhere on the grass, ordure extending far out from the rubbish chutes (with an acrid smell where ineffectual attempts had been made to burn it), broken glass, graffiti that never seemed to be witty. In contrast, the insides of the interviewees' flats were frequently – with some obvious exceptions – very clean and done up with great care with heavy immaculate wallpaper, sentimental pictures and objects, and gleaming white goods in the kitchen. Often there was a highly varnished, expensive front door, or a bell that played a trite but cheerful tune: gestures of demarcation from the collective anonymity outside, and generally several storeys up.

Representativeness

A very high priority often seems to have been placed on internal decoration in a very poor, sometimes destitute area; indeed, about a quarter to a third of the men interviewed were unemployed (even though the doorstep interview seeking was carried out on weekends or evenings). This is probably more or less representative; yet it seems quite surprising that only about a quarter of the women who were not of retirement age were jobless. This perhaps over-represents the extent to which traditional sex roles relating to employment have been eroded in the inner city.

In order to see whether those interviewed were obviously unrepresentative in their religious outlook, a simple numerical test was made at the end of the meeting (except in the case of the six covertly approached through the baptismal lists). A paper slip with 'How important is God in your life?' asked on it was given and read out; the eighteen interviewees were then asked to ring a scale from 1 ('not at all important') to 10 ('very important'). The overall average of 6.30 is identical, in terms of significant differences, with the average of 6.07 for social classes D and E recorded by a poll, apparently nationally representative, carried out by the Bible Society using Gallup fieldworkers. The increased importance of 'God' for those over 44–45 (7.20) compared to those under (5.00) also seems to be representative nationally, though the difference between men (6.00) and women (6.60) seems rather less than the national difference.[2] Though this test is probably misleading in suggesting the subjective significance of God, use of 'God' as a trigger word might be a valid indicator of general religious representativeness.

The mass media

Nearly everyone said they watched television a great deal ('I love television', etc.). This was evident on entering through the front door. 'Soaps' were the staple diet; films were said to be watched quite frequently; documentaries and the news were minority interests; and serious discussion programmes and anything to do with politics seemed hardly ever to be seen. Between about a fifth and a quarter of those interviewed said they watched religious services on TV. (There was no obvious difference between the quota and baptism samples.) A crippled man confined to a wheelchair said, 'I daren't use the phone between half-past six and eight o'clock'; a young upwardly mobile SDP voter said he did not watch *Coronation Street* but, from conversation at work and elsewhere, always knew what was happening in it. The fantasy community conveyed by television seems to have replaced vicinal community; and it would be surprising if the values implicit in television, which perhaps include materialism and middle-class individualist aspirations, have had no impact on the inner city.

The *Sun* was the most widely read newspaper, then the *Mirror*. The *Mail*, the *Sunday Mail*, the *Daily Telegraph*, the *Sunday Times* and the *Evening Standard* were each mentioned only once. Rather more newspapers – especially the *Mirror* – were read by the baptism than by the quota sample.

Ethnicity

Tower Hamlets has demarcations of smell. On the corridors, whatever the day, there would often lurk a stale, greasy reek of 'Sunday lunch'. To an Asian or West Indian (or to a middle-class researcher) such a marker of white working-class identity might well be offputting. Similarly, very many of the interviewees had nasal objections to the curry smell coming from the Bangladeshi and Asian addresses on the estates. (Asians were especially concentrated to the West of Tower Hamlets, particularly in Spitalfields, which with its traditional turnover of immigrants, such as Huguenots and East European Jews, is perhaps the nearest London approaches to the ethnic stratification of New York. Blacks were less in evidence.)

A cleaner from Bow said there were two immigrants, 'black and Indian', in her corridor, but it was the cleanest in the building: 'it's just the food [curry] that worries me'. Similar was a man who said he had never been colour prejudiced, but he did not like the smell of Bengalis, though it was not to do with 'them'. 'Cooking and all that. It's not their fault, it's a different culture, isn't it?' This use of the word 'culture', in the broad anthropological sense that it was used by Tylor rather than in the restricted, high-minded sense of Matthew Arnold, suggests the influence of liberal, relativistic values mediated through television. From comments such as these came as a sense of discrimination based on evidence, not on prejudice or prejudging. It is too easy to dismiss all negative comments as merely rationalisations of race hatred. Indeed, there seemed to be some identification with immigrants as fellow victims.

However, among many – perhaps most to some extent – violent forces under the surface were probably ready to well up through the fissures of racial difference. The frequently remarked-on thought structure of 'I am not racist but . . .' was used by about a third to a half of the twenty who were asked about or brought up race relations. This often conveyed prejudice, but not always. 'I'm not being whatsit but there is a lot of Indians here', the problem being that they do not do much cleaning. 'We're not racialist, it's just that, I mean [voice lowered] they're just dirty.' Complaints were also made about noise. (The policy of educated radicals, who do not themselves live in the estates, of integrating the races through forcing collisions of custom at that most spontaneous of places, the home, seems to allow race hatred the enormous propaganda advantage of being difficult to separate from fair comment: or so it would seem from the interviews.)

Great resentment was directed at council policy which, it was strongly felt, discriminated against indigenous white culture in favour of that of immigrants. A roadsweeper said: 'I can't call a Paki a Paki, a nigger a nigger. Violence is in the air . . . You've got the African, the Pakistanis, the Bengalis, you've got the Sikhs [and he mentioned 'the Boat People'], they've all got their different ways . . . I don't believe I should put my religion onto them, and they shouldn't put their religion onto me.' No one else's words were so forceful, but I sense he was a spokesman for the majority. An energetic woman who took on voluntary work with children expressed a common frustration: 'But we're only ratepayers and we're not allowed to say nothing.'

All too evident fear and disintegration were expressed by those isolated whites in mainly Bangladeshi estates who inched their doors open some time after my knock. (None of these had the confidence to be interviewed.) Apart from a woman too mad to be included in the survey, this seemed to be the greatest form of suffering I encountered in Tower Hamlets. Similarly, a black woman told me in despair and fear how for eight years she had been waiting for a transfer from the council so that, as an abandoned wife with thrombosis in her legs, she could be among her own people.[3]

The lintels of Bangladeshi doors were very frequently inscribed with what I took to be the first Pillar of Islam, the Kalimah: 'There is no god but God: Muhammad is the messenger of God.' It was a reminder of how Islam, unlike Protestant Christianity, is rooted in popular practice, and of its discreteness from white working-class mores.

Class

Where white working-class identity is increasingly defined in terms of ethnic awareness, it may be that class antagonism is lessening. The crippled man said, 'It's a very old saying that men in the area used to get drunk and attack policemen and say, "You dirty bugger. You'd put your own mother away." And that's I think the view of most East Enders.' But this was probably a rather old-fashioned view; as perhaps was the comment of an ex-jockey. 'It's true that East Enders stick together . . . We don't watch what we do, we enjoy ourselves,' unlike the middle and upper classes he had seen: in a club, the latter 'have to stand still. I think that's bad'. He explained, 'It's like a pack of wolves really . . . You feel more secure than if you're on your own.'

More people, where the police were mentioned, criticised them for not being effective enough, especially in relation to teenage violence (irrespective of colour). Neighbours were very often perceived as hostile – this seems to be traditional in the East End – in an environment that was especially threatening because the old communal bonds were largely gone.

The feelings of the upwardly mobile people in Tower Hamlets were perhaps expressed by a woman who said she had defrauded her employer for the sake of her son since 'this world is a fight for survival'. 'There's no change, and surely you want to better yourself, or better your children? . . . Screaming at their children; can't they call?

There's no finesse . . . But that probably sounds a betrayal on my part because I am an East End person. So I do feel a little bit of a traitor . . . But their behaviour is frightening to me. Look, this is all closed, all windows, doors bolted and barred. I don't mix with them. But I don't think I'm better. I just feel that I am different. [With all the graffiti on the walls] you could never invite anybody here, could you? I couldn't. The flats themselves are nice though, aren't they? The council have tried . . . but it's the building itself outside – the children, they behave badly: they destroy and destroy . . .'

Most did not seem to be upwardly mobile, but nevertheless there was a widespread sense that standards had dropped. The environment was a 'piss-hole'; or, as the voluntary worker said, 'people just shut their doors and don't want to know'. An unemployed young family man who said he had once owned lorries instanced the 'slaphazard' action of a caretaker who moved a bucket across the floor by kicking it. As well as blaming the council, there was also a sense, as the roadsweeper put it, that 'basically, you blame the working man'. Also, he said, 'you swallow' rather than retaliate to the provocation of gangs of youths. People displayed plenty of mettle as individuals but despaired of any solution at a social or political level.

Articulation

This varied greatly, but was only conceptual in the case of the most educated person, an unemployed man with seven 'O' levels who spent much time in the public library. Other minds, such as the crippled man's, were obviously rich and lively, sharp in the perception of particulars, but associative in the expression of thoughts, so that there would flow streams of clauses whose interrelationship was vague. Ambiguity, far from being perceived as a problem, sometimes seemed to be felt appropriate, as a fair rendering of reality. Others were tongue-tied and unhappy at inarticulacy. 'I believe in some things – like in the religion, you know what I mean, but er . . .' (in response to 'Do you believe in God?'). Many expressed anxiety about not being articulate: here it often seemed that thoughts could not be shaped for a lack of syntax and vocabulary. Somebody started, 'You can't say you don't believe in something if you don't practise it,' displayed confusion and abandoned the struggle to have this particular complex thought. Literalmindedness was almost invariable, but I did not sense as much socially induced inhibitive structure as preliminary reading – based on experience a decade or so past – had made me expect.[4]

Sometimes there were apparent inversions: as with (in relation to funerals) 'just throwing somebody in a hole and chucking them over the dirt'. Nonce words were very frequent: such as, 'you know what I mean?'; 'and that'; and '-like' as a suffix. Possibly there was more body language than with middle-class English people, and it sometimes had culturally distinctive expressions (for example, the roadsweeper clicked his fingers).

Christianised culture unconsciously played a part in the casual vocabulary: for example, not knowing you 'from Adam'; or, 'when my mother was alive, God bless her soul' (the speaker when directly asked was ambivalent about, or an unbeliever in, the existence of God). Blasphemy and profanities were probably unusually infrequent because of my presence and that of the tape recorder. Protestant culture seemed to have taken root in so far that there seemed to be a general presumption in favour of thinking for oneself; but the result of this did not appear to be an appreciative identification with the established church.

'THEM', or ATTITUDES TOWARDS CHURCH OF ENGLAND CULTURE AND CHRISTIANITY

Rites de passage

'Everybody had a christening,' said the crippled man. It has already been seen how, within the self-selection of the interviewees, diffusion of the rite made the demarcation between the quota and baptism samples fairly meaningless. Only about a third of the quota were clearly indifferent to baptism, or secularist; and some in the baptism sample were also. In the baptism sample, in about half the cases, one spouse, nearly always the woman, was obviously more in favour of the christening than the other.

It is difficult to plumb the sense of rightness about christening. My impression is that it has power as a traditional action (rather than belief), set apart from everyday life, that focuses on that most altruistic of natural impulses, the nurture of children. The sprinkling of water seems to bring together pragmatic, communal, ethical and metaphysical realities.

Pragmatically, there is, as the SDP voter and others pointed out, schooling to consider; he preferred Church of England schools not because of 'religion' but because he thought they provided a relatively high standard of education and discipline. There seems also to be some symbiosis between the *rites de passage*. A bingo-loving grandmother said, 'If you're going to get married, you'd have to be baptised before you get married.' There also seems to be some sense that christening is about naming, and that without it communal identity is not legitimated; perhaps this is why most people seemed to use the word 'christening' rather than 'baptism'. (It was not my impression that the difference between sprinkling and immersion prompted this usage.)

A moral and metaphysical association was also expressed. The unemployed man who had once owned lorries had had his children christened 'because it's a certain amount of belief in God, isn't it?, I suppose. They've got to grow to respect other people, and things like that. If you aren't christened at all, then you ain't got no belief in nothing, have you? So we christened the children, I suppose, because, I dunno . . .' The bingo-loving grandmother said, 'in the eyes of God . . . it's the name . . . it's blessed.'

In teasing out these strands of identification with christening, it would almost certainly be incorrect to suggest that the bond is still generally strong. A woman's 'Oh yeah' to 'Were your children baptised?' sounded as if the reply was really 'of course'; but against those like this traditionally minded, elderly Spitalfields woman should be set the many others who seemed to be more in tune with a middle-aged man who said his children were christened more 'as a tradition than anything else'. (He had to consult his wife to find out whether they had been christened.)

White weddings in church have been 'bred in us' (the Spitalfields woman). A Stepney man in physical training said that he would have preferred a marriage in church in white, especially for his wife, but could not afford it. The expense of what is deemed to go properly with a church as opposed to Registry Office wedding was mentioned by quite a few. However, a sixteen year old girl on a youth training scheme said, 'I don't think it makes much difference.'

The crippled man said, 'I know it's supposed to be God and *blessing* the wedding, but I feel very much that they don't really do that, they think of the bride in white and all the trimmings!' For him whiteness and virginity were still strongly associated: he became ribald about – it seems, in his childhood – mothers who even sent 'them down the aisle six months pregnant with a big bouquet to hide it'.

However, the religious underpinning provided by a wedding in church seemed to be in the minds of some. A Bethnal Green mother expressed this in terms of a negative relationship, seeming to feel it hypocritical for a non-believer to marry in church ('If you never go, it's a bit, you know'). Linked with this is the erosion of marriage as an institution. The roadsweeper said, 'I mean, even your marriages are a fallacy now. I'm married and believe in marriage.'

An inarticulate young wife's only comment of consequence was in relation to funerals: 'That's the only time we see the inside of a church.' Cremating instead of burying has probably diluted the significance of the ceremony. The stigma associated with the former has now, it seems, been outweighed by the expense of the latter. Somebody said, 'My mum said before she died, "Don't burn me." I don't care. Do what you like with me.' One man who visited the grave of his father felt 'he's still there'; but the Bethnal Green mother's attitude was probably more representative: 'I don't care what they do. They can put me in a plastic bag and stick me down the chute, you know what I mean?'

Whatever the mode of disposal, there is some feeling in favour of last rites. The Stepney man in training, who rated God as of very low importance in his life, nevertheless said that a religious funeral service was 'quite important really'. A lift engineer who thought of himself as non-religious (he was fascinated by science fiction of the van Daniken sort) said, 'We have to go to weddings and funerals, and it makes it all a little bit more easier to take . . . Just a ceremony that lightens the thing for somebody.' A trainee taxi-driver, who was eager to bring up his children outside Tower Hamlets, said, 'Weddings, christenings, burial, and that's me lot.'

That it is communally embedded action in relation to natural events, rather than belief in relation to supernatural events, that makes sense to Tower Hamlets people is illustrated by a woman who said she saw nothing special in Jesus but also said, 'I do believe in Christmas.' The word 'believe' here relates to practice, not faith. Christmas Eve mass (not the more specifically Christian Easter) seemed to be the occasion most likely to see occasional church attendance from these non-attenders; Christmas appears to be very important in the East End (and elsewhere) as a carnival with a natural centre, the family. Perhaps some immanent presence is conveyed by carols and candles (the latter seem to be of considerable importance as a link between the natural and the numinous).

Given that the *rites de passage*, though diffused among those interviewed, do not seem to evoke much enthusiasm, it is probably significant that about four people objected to the recent and patchy practice in Tower Hamlets of making administration of the rites of baptism and marriage conditional on promises of church attendance. 'He *had* to go, which I find is a bit of hypocrisy,' said a man of his about to be married son. Another man said, 'I don't think it's right at all. I don't think they should insist.' Again, 'The church makes so many stipulations . . . There's a bag of sweets for sixpence if you're prepared to give a shilling for it.' (This may not have been connected with church attendance.) However, the ex-jockey and the trainee taxi-driver (perhaps reflecting the exclusivism of white working-class culture) seemed to feel that such restrictive policies were proper.

The roadsweeper developed a theologically interesting critique: 'I said to the preacher when I had my baby baptised,[1] "I don't go to church." He said, "Well, I'm not baptising." I said, "Why not?" He said, "You don't go to church." I think it's wrong . . . I let them go to church if they *want to go* to church, but no way will I make my children go to church . . . [That is] basically what they're saying. [The children will then say they have been forced.] He said I don't go to church. I said, "What's that to do with that?" I said, "I'm asking you to baptise my child." I said, "*I* don't believe in it, there's nothing to say my child don't believe in it" . . . To me, baptism is a key to the door, to church . . . Every man and every woman has got a mind of its own, and you've got to use that mind . . . They've still got to use their own mind, but that mind's got to come from the beginning. You've got to put that little seed there . . .'

Church of England services

The *rites de passage* are still, to a considerable extent, 'us' as well as 'them'; but Church of England services seem to be unambiguously 'them'. Only a few were not eligible as interviewees because they attended services. Yet five-sixths of those interviewed, in giving preliminary 'routine' facts, placed themselves as 'C. of E.' (not 'Anglican', with its intellectualist, aesthetic, upper middle-class connotations).[2]

Probably about a third overall – perhaps more like a half of the quota sample – were decided non-churchgoers (apart from *rites de passage*). 'Too much bleeding church don't do you any good,' said a retired baker who had been brought up in a Church of England children's home. Very untypical was the woman who – though not really a churchgoer nevertheless! – said services had been improved in her local church: 'It's not quite so hard . . . They're lighter in their speech, very much lighter . . . It's more interesting than when we was going. It's more like a friendship speaking, as if everybody's got close together . . .' Several people who took non-attendance for granted seemed to have no thoughts about ways in which Church of England services could be improved.

It was often said – especially by the baptism sample – that church was boring: 'they're always so *gloomy*, boring'; and, the preaching 'would get me down . . . It's boring, and I think to myself, a lot of it's a load of old twaddle'; the sixteen year old girl felt services were 'boring', as did the Stepney man in training; the roadsweeper said that 'our churches' were 'boring . . . you can enjoy a bloody good sleep in them'; or, proceedings were 'churchified' (this woman had been to a Methodist service which was 'very informal'). The unemployed man with seven 'O' levels thought 'the priest has got to radiate something, be a very good speaker, be very, very clear'. The crippled man said, 'I don't get nothing from church. Have you ever been to a badly acted play?' At church once with 'the pastor trying to play the organ, choir all at a different tempo', he 'thought, "God, what am I doing here?" . . . I know they're all trying their best, but for me it wasn't good enough . . . I'm so good at preaching at other people and don't get on with preachers. I don't have his point of view anyway.' Most people do not go to church, he said, they 'watch the goggle box'.

Cultural embarrassment was another factor. 'I don't feel comfortable. I don't feel as if I belong there . . . I'm not a very good reader either.' The retired baker said of services, 'I can't keep up with them.' The ex-jockey said, 'I mean, they've got their congregation, all the people there . . . You walk in, you're a stranger really, because no one knows you, you don't know no one else . . . It's hard just to walk into a church I think these days . . . You get a fuddy duddy old woman who makes a fuss about it. You'd get the one . . . People who don't go to church don't know the hymns, they're too frightened to sing . . . People who do go to church, they're all raring to go, singing.' After 'his mate's boy's christening', said the man who had once owned lorries, about half the congregation came round and 'shook our hand and all that sort of thing: "Thanks for coming." That . . . embarrasses me.' There was also some feeling that it was 'not quite the done thing' for a man to go to church (unless perhaps a Catholic). A woman who had been in a 'nerve' hospital said that the reason most people do not go to church is fear of what the neighbours would say (others also suggested this). But the taboo is possibly weaker than it used to be; certainly, people said it did not apply to *their* opinions.

Other reasons for non-attendance included the association of church with dead people (from the sixteen year old girl); because some people who go to church 'do harm, murder, don't they?'; and the belief that church attendance was linked with a fear of not going to heaven because of non-attendance. Services on television, however, seem to have been watched, or, at least, not switched off, by quite a few.

Gospel-type services were brought up and praised by four people. 'I prefer to see coloured people at church because it's quite entertaining', someone said. The Spitalfields woman, echoing her husband, said she liked 'Hallelujah coloured-type services'. The roadsweeper was once near what he wanted to call 'niggers' at a Gospel dance 'and do you know what, I bloody enjoyed it . . . their way of doing it'. The Stepney man in training said, 'Gospel-type church is more interesting, more lively. That's basically why a lot of people don't go [to Church of England services]: it's the same thing, week in, week out.'

The vicar

About three-quarters of the quota sample had never seen their local Church of England vicar, and over a half had never been aware of a Church of England vicar of any kind.

One man, an Anglo-Burmese bachelor with eleven cats, was attending a Methodist church because, he said, he did not know where the Anglican church was. About three people were aware of their Church of England vicar; two were negative about him.

In contrast, out of the half of the baptism sample who had seen their local vicar, five were positive about him, and none obviously negative. (This leaves out of account adverse comments on strict baptism and wedding policies.) It may be that the visibility of the clergy tends to be positively correlated with acceptance of them.

Most positive of all the responses: 'If it wasn't for a priest [Church of England] I think I'd go mad.' Also, the vicar was 'ever so nice, very nice chap'; and a 'nice bloke . . . He knew we weren't all churchgoers so he gave us a lecture afterwards [i.e., after the baptism] . . . He was having a knock at us, wasn't he? Bloke ain't stupid, is he?' The roadsweeper approved of a working-class laypreacher who spoke '"Oh hello, aw sod you." Now to hear a bloke of that description say that . . . a preacher *swearing* . . . He said, "I'm just one of you." He was . . . And that I liked . . . I like arguments. If a churchman comes down here . . . I'd invite him in, not to take the mickey, but you can learn . . . I thought to myself, "I can enjoy you."'

The two who were negative about vicars they knew reacted against apparent rejection. The sixteen-year girl said she did not like her vicar for 'when I stopped going to Sunday school he wouldn't say "hello" or anything . . .' (To please her most, a vicar would need to be 'old and kind'.) A mature capable woman who has already been mentioned said she had, when in distress, tried approaching the local Church of England vicar. 'I've been dismissed, well, not dismissed, but they talk [She put on a parody of an upper middle-class throaty accent: the man underneath it could well have been in full retreat from the emotionality of an energetic, disturbed woman], "Yes, yes, well, why, er" – they go like that. In other words, you're dismissed, you know: "I've got something else to do." ' Later, she said it was almost as if vicars are saying 'my time is valuable'. She said she was converting to Catholicism and always kept a candle burning.

Being visible probably amounts to more than just being there: one woman said she did not come across the vicar at all, and that the only time she saw him was when she went to jumble sales. More general comments on vicars included: 'They sort of help people, don't they? . . . I do know vicars that go out drinking. And smoke as well. They're quite pleasant. Tell dirty jokes and things like that.' The ex-jockey seemed to approve of a vicar who (in connection with a *rite de passage*) was 'trying to put one at ease, you know what I mean. He started laughing and joking and all that.' (But later he added, 'If the vicar knocks on the door, usually you decide . . . a collection. People haven't usually got the money to give them but they do, just out of the kindness of their hearts . . . Most people don't want them to get involved . . . They can't really help you, can they? Some people like to keep their own private lives to themselves.') The crippled man said: 'Vicars are nice, pleasant people. They believe wholly in what they're doing. They're *vicars*! Unless you're a churchgoer you don't give it much thought. They're "them people", you know what I mean? Like me, they're strange.'

Visits did not seem to be discouraged: for example, the Spitalfields woman and the woman who had been in a 'nerve' hospital said they would receive their local vicars. The latter, however, also said, 'Some of them are all right, but from what I read in the papers, some of them can be worse than what we are . . . Some of them interfere with children, don't they? So they're not all goody-goodies.' She attacked a Church of England vicar who had talked about 'the atom bomb' to old people in a club ('stupid' to frighten old people). Asked what was the best way a vicar could behave, she reacted as to an odd question: 'Well, just an ordinary man, I should imagine – like . . . Do good, I suppose. Come round and talk with you, or something like that . . . We give Jehovah's Witnesses tea.'[3]

Two men who were opposed to religion did not seem opposed to visits: the retired baker said merely that if the local vicar knocked on the door 'he would not convert me'; the lift engineer fascinated by science fiction said the vicar is 'just another person as far as I'm concerned', though 'you might watch your ps and qs when you're talking to him'. (He said he was no longer afraid of those kind of people.) 'I think they should socialise more . . . [and] . . . drop this black cloak business.'

The Church of England

Judging from the many opinions expressed about the established church, it has a considerably more negative image than the vicar who is locally visible. In part at least, this negativity seems to be conditioned by the past. Those who have had a child baptised were generally less negative. There seems to have been no difference between the sexes, or between those under and those over forty-five years old.

The Bethnal Green mother quoted her grandfather on the First World War, 'They used to bless you and send you out to be killed.' The retired baker, whose Church of England children's home made him go to church every Sunday, saw all the churches as 'bloody hypocrites'. The crippled man criticised the church for – over two decades ago – being 'patronising to the young people, the Rock stars and so forth'.

'Church-type people' struck the sixteen year old girl as being like a friend who 'seems really lonely . . . always reading books . . . I don't think it's [the church is] a happy place.' The ex-jockey, along with some others, seemed to see the church as rich and powerful. 'I think the church should step in to end poverty altogether. In the House of Commons they [the church] do have a say, and they are for the poor . . . I don't think God really meant me to be poor, to live a life of hell.'

From the baptism sample came, 'I've got nothing against the churches'; and 'I feel nothing' about the Church of England; and 'seems to me they're just business people in a way'. The roadsweeper said: 'I don't knock the church. If you go home and pray to the moon, that's up to you, or the totem pole, or whatever you do, it's your choice.'

Even the woman who said she would go mad if it was not for a priest only said of the church: 'It means quite a lot to me.' This was the only positive comment from someone who did not seem to be nudging a middle-class status. The SDP voter said: 'The church helps a lot of people and for them it's good, the people who need that kind of help.' After referring to Henry VIII and the Borgias, he commented: 'You start to wonder, is it the blind leading the blind?' The man with seven 'O' levels said the Church of England is 'very necessary, very useful, very sane, very beneficial. Those that have faith usually succeed. The Church of England must teach people how to acquire confidence.' The only reader of the *Daily Mail* said: 'I do believe in the church but I don't go, so therefore it suits me as things are. They [her husband and children] go regular [to the Roman Catholic church] and we both keep our religions.'

The routine self-descriptions as Church of England by five-sixths of the interviewees, and the considerable evidence of further links through Church of England schools, some Sunday school and the *rites de passage*, sit strangely with the reactions to the Church of England when brought up as a trigger word or in some neutrally expressed question (something like, 'What do you think of the Church of England?'). Though class[4] was the blind spot of this research, it seems likely from the more inferential context that the 'them'/'us' dichotomy is the main factor in this ambivalence. This is evident architecturally: the Hawksmoor churches, the Victorian spires, even the spirituality

of a postwar church built out of modern brick, proclaim
Anglicanism, a set apart, aesthetically and intellectually
incomprehensible establishment, now miniaturised by the
gross collectivism of the grid of estates across Tower
Hamlets. The recent mosque in the Whitechapel Road is in
total contrast: despite the alien cultural style of Islam, the
building, of a jarring brick with shop space in the front, has
a popularist feel that belongs. Even the Catholic churches,
with their (sometimes coloured) images and solid look, do
not seem so marked out. Apart from St Dunstan's, which
seemed still to conjure up some folk awareness, Church of
England buildings did not appear to be much in people's
minds.[5]

There may be a mental mechanism by which established
Anglicanism is bracketed off from the Church of England
as some sort of semi-conscious ascriptive identity. Initia-
tion into a religion seems often to be seen in terms of rite or
ascriptiveness rather than of mere belief. Thus a young man
described himself as 'Church of England and Mormon',
though he said the Mormons were 'con artists'; he had been
baptised a Mormon during his teens. An elderly woman
said she was Church of England – though she had been
brought up a Catholic – because her husband was Church
of England (he was present). The Spitalfields woman initially described herself as Church of England though
(probably like very many middle-class members) thinking
'when you're at school they say Jesus was the Son of God
. . . and then you think to yourself "no" – like.' Doctrine
per se, even where it is crucial to Anglican identity, tempor-
arily halted even the intelligent, television-bound crippled
man's flow of conversation: 'The Bishop of Durham caused
quite a lot of controversy about the, um . . . I don't know
what he was on about . . . the Resurrection, sorry . . .'

The Church of England headed by the Queen may have
some sort of resonance as a 'civil religion',[6] a kind of
'religion' that falls short of the supernatural, and is also
distinct from the type of patriotism that is the last refuge of

a scoundrel (or racist): its core would be feeling for 'the British way of life'. But there was some ambivalence about the Royal Family, though they were largely regarded positively at the same time. Perhaps 'them'/'us' feeling was behind this impression of distance. The Royal Family 'are all right. I think they do a great job' perhaps reflects the consensus (a large majority of the interviewees commented). A few obviously were closely identified, and also there was some undertow: 'I think they should keep the Duke and the Queen but not the other hangers on, you know what I mean?'

The Bible

The embeddedness of Christianity in even contemporary language can be glimpsed by the references to the Bible. Half of each sample related themselves to it, even though no question was directly asked. Yet no one said they read it. The crippled man declared, 'There's no way I'm going to sit down and read the Bible, because I get nothing from it.' (He used to select passages at random.) There was also great literal mindedness about it. In Tower Hamlets there is no social practice – among whites – like that of the Five Pillars of Islam, the means by which Muhammad instilled his religion of the word (and, later, Book) into non-readers, himself included. This absence encourages random, idiosyncratic internalisations.

The Stepney man in training said of Adam and Eve, 'It's incest, isn't it?' The woman who had been in a 'nerve' hospital joked literally about Eve: 'If she didn't tempt him with an apple we'd all be good.' The Bethnal Green mother, questioning why God let little children suffer, cited 'Suffer the little children and that or whatever.' The lift engineer fascinated by science fiction suggested – *inter alia* – that Samson's strength could be explained if he came from a space-craft (his voice became closely involved). The ex-jockey said, 'I think the Bible is a book written many years ago, just like a book we would write.'

There seemed to be only two references that related to the 'Anglican' level of culture. The Anglo-Burmese man had a theological difficulty in relation to God calling Jesus his son, since he also is coequally God; and a man said, 'Things it's got in the Bible, it's all coming true . . . There's going to be another war and that . . .' He had been visited by Jehovah's Witnesses but denied any influence. These were also unusual in being references to the New Testament.

The Bible was also commented on as an authority on morals. The trainee taxi-driver saw what the Bible stands for as 'quite good . . . I've not read all the Bible but I know basically it's got good intentions, hasn't it? Good standards.' The roadsweeper said that no man or woman could live with the ten commandments today.

Ultimate beliefs

Though Protestantism seems to have caused some rooting of individualism in Tower Hamlets (and television is probably topping up the culture with its modern variant, liberal pluralism), emphasis on belief as such in any analytical sense was generally absent. Asked if they believed in God, the interviewees did not (in their own words distinguish between theism and pantheism, or bring up creation, omnipotence, omniscience, human free will and so on as themes. It was as if 'God' was taken for granted as a word and to *think* about it was strange.[7]

There was more 'belief in God' than in other Christian ultimates, such as the divinity of Jesus and the existence of life after death. Few people denied the existence of God; the greatest disbelief, though more of a 'religious' than a secularist kind, came from some upper working-class men in the *baptism* sample. (Perhaps relatively pious women attracted them.) The consensus was probably doubting belief, an ambiguity closer to experience than to conceptual rigour. Perhaps it was the impact of experience that made a good quarter of the replies develop into less positive statements. 'Well, there's only one God in the world . . . We don't see him.' No reference was made specifically to the Holy Spirit.

Some exceptionally differentiated statements included a reference to free will, and a distinction between 'God' and 'some great power' (in which the lift engineer believed). The Bethnal Green mother said, 'It's all according to what you think God is. You can't imagine a God sitting up there [laughs].' Three outsiders, the crippled man, the Anglo-Burmese, and the unemployed man with seven 'O' levels ('I believe in a power within everybody which I call the subconscious . . . The difficulty is in getting hold of it'), were also much more sophisticated than the others.

Their statements included fatalism (hardly predestination): 'I just believe there's a God of some sorts [laughs] I'm not too deeply into it – I just think there's something else that kind of moves us about and guides whatever your destiny. We take a path we don't really want to travel and yet we find ourselves on it . . .' 'God' was affirmed through denying 'atheism' and 'Allah'. A naive psychological analogy was used: 'I think if you can pray to somebody he must be there.' The 'Almighty' was also 'the only one I'd turn to . . . for the strength to come back again' if 'I'm really down'. Prayer was mentioned by very many, seemingly largely in the context of asking for favours for oneself or others at times of hardship or distress. There was no 'Anglican' wordiness about taking a 'mature' view of an ineffable God.

Doubt was only once scientific (the lift engineer fascinated by science fiction); and only once expressed through psychological insight (the SDP voter said people only want to believe in God because they would like to believe there is someone who is going to help them). Experience of suffering was much more important. (Here 'God' implicitly seems to be identified with an omnipotent being of love and compassion, not as a God, such as Allah, who transcends good and evil.) At least three-eighths of the interviewees were spontaneous in linking God to the experience of suffering or evil. 'I believe there's somebody there but then he's looking down in funny ways, he's doing things in funny ways.'

'It's hard to believe when you see all this suffering in the world,' said the 'nerve' hospital woman; the lift engineer said, 'I don't believe that if there was a God he could be so mean'; the road sweeper said, 'You've got Ethiopia'; the bingo-loving grandmother mentioned 'child murderers', saying, 'and you say, "Where is God?"' Other people said: 'Our first boy died of leukaemia. If there is a God, why let a child like that suffer?'; and, 'You're supposed to be with God all the time. So if you're with God, why are you suffering now?' The suffering mentioned related more to sympathy with others than to the self, and tended to be natural rather than obviously caused by human agency.

Some referred to pain expressed through religious allegiance. 'I think religion causes a lot of trouble, you know. The Irish and all that.' The Bethnal Green mother spoke of 'India: one lot went into the temple.' The cultural pluralism of television news seems to encourage a pessimistic impartiality.

Evil as an almost numinous force was only mentioned by the woman who said she had defrauded her employer: in prison with a child murderess, 'I had a good look into her eyes. She really looks evil, which I found sad because I thought, "You cannot help that." On the surface she's trying very hard to be good. But it'll beat her in the end, this evilness. She's not mad though.' She wondered if this was the devil, or to be understood psychologically. But generally suffering was not linked with evil to produce a symbiosis with theistic salvationist belief.

A positive link between suffering and the ultimate was

suggested by only two people, both outsiders: the crippled man said 'God only gives you the cross to carry that you're able to carry'; and the Anglo-Burmese was the only subject to relate suffering to a Jesus who saves ('Jesus came to suffer what man suffered. He degraded himself'). The only other person to bring up Jesus in the context of suffering saw him 'as a human being really . . . not so much as a God'.

Only about a quarter of the interviewees seem to have believed Jesus was the Son of God. A naturalistic theme emerged: 'I believe-like he was there.' Jesus was 'just an ordinary person'; stories about him 'could be by Enid Blyton' (the Bethnal Green mother); and, 'He might have been a madman for all they know, and they believed in him. It's like that Billy Graham, because everyone believes that he's something really good, don't they?' The retired baker said it is 'only people's imagination that Jesus is the Son of God . . . Virgin Mary a virgin? No, my foot [laughs]. You must be joking. How can she be a virgin if she had a child? [laughs] I've put you on the spot, haven't I?'[8] There was also an ethical theme; and even an ethical analogy: Jesus was God 'for all the good work he's done'.

Both samples seem to have been evenly split on the question of whether or not there is life after death, with roughly a third believing, a third disbelieving and the other third doubting. 'I believe there is a hereafter. But I don't know what it is. I just don't think. I don't puzzle me brains,' said the wife from Spitalfields. Three believed in reincarnation (the Anglo-Burmese, the lift engineer and the man who said he had once owned lorries).[9] The roadsweeper did not believe 'in knocking' life after death because of one of his children's psychic experience. Incertitude was expressed by the bingo-loving grandmother ('Oh, I don't know about that') and the sixteen year old girl ('Well, I've never encountered it'). Down to earth disbelief was expressed thus: 'Once you're dead you're dead. You can't come back again'; and, 'Once you're gone you're gone.'

(One of these was converting to Catholicism, the other was a 'Christian'.) The cleaner from Bow, after saying, perhaps dubiously, 'I think when you're gone you're gone', laughed knowingly as if she surpassed holy black, like Crazy Jane.[10]

In a survey carried out in 1968 in almost adjacent Islington (but not just among the working classes) it was found that 60% said they looked at horoscopes, and a third did so regularly (and that working-class people were much more inclined to read the horoscope). Furthermore, 9–23% really believed in aspects of astrology. Only 6–8% really believed in the efficacy of other superstitions.[11] Similarly, slightly more of both the quota and baptism samples seem to have read their horoscopes than not; and no more than a quarter of those answering (i.e., all the twenty-four interviewees) seemed to have had partial belief or more. In Tower Hamlets the disbelief was generally rational, like that of the retired baker who rejected both newspaper and breakfast television horoscopes since 'every paper you bring up is always different versions to what other people's has'. This scepticism, as with that considered proper by the Greeks when interpreting oracles, may have been about human motives distorting a potentially true message. However, the general attitude seemed to be that the newspaper horoscope was 'just a bit of fun', or consulted for 'laughs and jokes with a friend'; or 'it's always not really serious so I don't mind reading it'.[12]

'THEM' ON 'US', AND 'THEM' ON 'THEM': ANGLICAN CLERGY IN TOWER HAMLETS

It was not always easy to find the vicarage. Together with the church and associated buildings it generally formed an enclave belonging to the style of the minor gentry and professional classes in pre-industrial and Victorian England. Inside, there tended also to be a complete contrast with the interiors of the flats on the estates. The vicarage front room was typically furnished plainly and inexpensively, often with 'common room' armchairs, in the decent, almost threadbare idiom of the vocational educated classes before the impact of the consumer society. Here was 'Anglicanism'.

The meetings, from which notes were taken, were with the twelve clergy who had nominated estates and were asked for baptism lists.[1]

'Them' on 'us': or the clergy on the Tower Hamlets white working-class

Religion

A good half of the twelve clergy seem to have thought there was a diffuse theism which fell short of being Christian. The

doubt and ambiguity expressed by many of the interviewees were not expressly predicted by the clergy, only
two of whom spontaneously linked belief in God to the
experience of suffering or evil. Appropriately, few mentioned Jesus in relation to belief. Life after death was also
little instanced.

The clergy had been asked what folk or implicit religion
they thought there was. Only one mentioned reincarnation. About a quarter brought up spiritualism and a few
spoke of prayer, astrology, candles, the occult and magic.[2]
It was striking how far the responses were anecdotal rather
than analytical.

Tower Hamlets culture

They seemed more at home in conveying the feel of Tower
Hamlets than in describing folk or implicit religion. For
example, there is an 'anticlericalism in Bethnal Green
which you don't find in Poplar'. There was said to be a
'presence' in one incumbent's area, but not in all Tower
Hamlets. Security may have been found by some in the
ancientness of many of the churches, predating as they do
'Tower Hamlets', the 'East End' and industrialism and in
part even the Stuarts and Norman Conquest. The war and
Bethnal Green, and the Anglo-Catholic tradition, are
living history.

There was a strong sense of the erosion of white working-
class community. This was attributed mainly to the pre-
dominance of GLC estates, with an influx of white problem
families from other London areas. The indigenous whites
'keep their balconies clean', but the whites coming in
'would not respond to carol singing'. Television was little
mentioned; but at least two clergymen said that people
were not as working class as they were. 'They're prepared
to think differently, even politically – they're swinging
towards the Liberals (not the SDP).' Immigration and
racial prejudice were much on the clergy's minds. The large

number of Bangladeshis in his parish seemed to lead one
clergyman into thinking that white people were virtually
unobtainable (they were surely the largest ethnic group).

Also, there was a strong sense of there being no change.
The culture was 'the same as Charles Booth's "empty
churches and complete indifference"'. A clergyman with a
relatively large congregation was rather exceptional in
providing psychological insight: traditional East Enders
are 'flamboyant, emotional, full of fun . . . There is a
macho image, but they are softies underneath. The joke
sees them through.' Many mentioned female leadership;
an experienced visitor stated, 'I always have to make
consultation with the wife first of all.' Also brought up by
one was the importance of 'nan', the grandmother. One
clergyman said that 'the hardest group (apart from the
Muslims) is the happy, successful working-class man' who
is 'friendly but would resist any pressure to express inward
belief'.

'There's a lot of respect for the fact that I'm a vicar here
. . . At the same time it goes with a sort of debunking as
well. There's a love/hate relationship with the church.'
Class and the problem of clerical role seemed to be generally perceived, through long experience, as posing insoluble
dilemmas. 'Church people here read the *Mirror* and the
Star rather than the *Sun*', and, 'Our churchwarden reads
the *Mail*'; '"Say one for me" is an important phrase – it
implies you believe in God more clearly than I do, and you
go to church, so you can intercede on my behalf'; 'If people
don't go to church, it's still the Church of England they
don't go to.' There is a 'basic feeling that the church is out
for money'. Some referred to a taboo on churchgoing, and
the church building was perceived ambivalently by clergy
as productive of both intimidation and numinous awe.

There was a consensus about the need to avoid a phoney
identification with white working-class culture. ('Cockneys
can't stand "'ampstead Cockneys"'). A distinction between paternalism and condescension also seemed to be

implicit. There was accord with a clergyman of working-class origins who said, 'Vicars are not wanted to be the same as people generally in the parish.' It seemed to be assumed that 'people obviously react to vicars in religious ways'.

Communicating Christianity

That 'belief' might be culturally alien to white working-class mentality did not seem to be stressed. There was a sense of strain. 'You get into the habit of repeating things. People are not trained to listen'; 'I explain words that are difficult by saying it's inconsequential'; 'Tower Hamlets people give you the answer you want to hear.' A clergyman with a relatively large congregation said, 'Half the business is being able to relate.'

There was some evidence for a positive correlation between larger congregations and an emphasis on the need for a personal relationship with parishioners. A clergyman who claimed his congregation had considerably increased cited the adage that a visiting priest makes for a full congregation; another with a large congregation referred to evangelistic efforts (though 'sporadic') and said, 'I think we're bad at spreading Christianity.' In contrast, two clergymen with small congregations said: 'People look for privacy and want to be on their own . . . I haven't much experience of door to door visiting – "I've come to talk about God"'; and, 'I let people approach me. I sometimes go into a pub.' A well-thought-out variant from a clergyman who claimed a sudden 'take off' in attendance: 'We don't do house to house visiting. We have an ongoing teaching ministry', with 'lay people themselves foremost in evangelism. "Like to like" is the best principle. Our task is to help the laity to be the ministry.' (It was difficult to find the vicarage.) Presumably, if this strategy works, a powerful relationship between the vicar and the lay evangelisers will have been established. It would seem that both conscious paternalism and strong anti-paternalism are compatible with increasing attendance; the sense of being convinced is probably helpful.

Baptism policy

This varied from open to very strict, with a preponderance somewhere in the middle: for example, after referring to twenty-seven reports commissioned on baptism since the 1920s, a clergyman saw it as the fault of the church to have neglected preparation in the past. He said, 'I insist on a minimal church attendance and preparation groups.'

In one parish there has been a very strict policy with an insistence that parents come to church. 'I've been astonished that seems to work. We work towards their coming to church afterwards. It's successful, about fifty per cent continue coming to church. Most of the growth of the congregation comes from this.' The success in relation to those whose connection with the *rite de passage* was thereby severed was not specified.

A clergyman on the open side said, 'I now feel there's a negative use of power over baptism, now the church is in decline.' The open policy was justified theologically by another as to do with the gifts of God for the baby and 'not at all to do with the faith of the parents. Baptism is potential membership . . . through sign and symbol.' (The roadsweeper had his own way of saying much the same.)

Theological accord was not evident. Finesse is needed to reconcile 'I don't often come across the superstitious idea that if a child is not baptised it's in danger' with 'I think something happens during baptism.' The latter view is probably a minority one however. The speaker reconciled it with the sectarian tendency towards an exclusive baptism policy by saying that harm is done if a child is exposed to grace and nothing is done about it.

'Them' on 'them': or the clergy on themselves

Orthodoxy

Many of the clergy thought that a high proportion of the others in Tower Hamlets were strongly orientated towards the social gospel; but only two seemed obviously that way in the meeting[3] (and only one of these seemed to be beyond any possible distinctively Christian orthodoxy). This probably indicates conflict between the *de jure* and the *de facto*, rather than a conscious assimilation of the *de jure* by the *de facto*. The social gospel in question seems generally to be concentrated on opposing racism and a nuclear defence policy: it reflects 'them', a brew of passionately idealistic liberalism with more than a dash of genteel socialism added in. This 'issue' consciousness, which in terms of a pastoral vocation seems to some over-theoretical and excessively secular, probably results from the collision of two cultural forces: 'Anglicanism', and what appears to be the uncongenial reality of the white working classes.

A question was asked about eschatology rather than the incarnation since, in the limited time available, immanentisation of (or lack of concern about) the eschaton seemed likely to be a more adequate indicator of social utopianism *de jure* than trying to pin down statements about the uniqueness of Christ.

About a third were broadly evangelical (stressing more than the others the biblical, fully Persian – or Persian-type – eschatology). One used the caterpillar–chrysalis–butterfly analogy[4] to illustrate Jesus' transforming return in power and glory, judgment, the new heaven, the new earth; he pointed out that in the gospels Jesus refers to hell as many as thirteen times. The two others, however, seemed also to see 'doing a fairly good job in caring for people' (as one put it) as an end in itself.

Nearly half were broadly Catholic (two at least were explicitly Anglo-Catholic). They seemed to be moderate socialists, or liberal-radicals (with perhaps only one quite conservative). The Persian, cosmic dimension of eschatology was generally much less stressed than it was by the evangelically inclined, but a minimal amount remained (about as much as in the Judaism that was not influenced by the intertestamental literature). Hell as 'eternal torment from a God of Love' was generally avoided: instead, for example, hell is knowledge of the absence of God; or indeed, is when 'the old girl [in hospital] can't reach the window that is blowing down her neck . . . it has eternal significance'; or (it seems) hell is selective absence of the afterlife. Many, perhaps most, of the clergy, who were delightfully individual, did not 'slot' easily into any ideal-types; for example, one clergyman identified with the liberalism of the late nineteenth century, but not with its optimism.

Several stressed the reality of evil. Only two seemed in any way identified with psychology (one with psychology as a philosophical perspective; the other had some Jungian affinities). There was perhaps some feeling that in Tower Hamlets theology was the sort of luxurious overview that only a visiting sociologist could indulge in. A clergyman in jeans with a big buckled belt said, 'We're not going to get too heavy with the resurrection, are we, this afternoon?'

Other clergy

Very many seemed to feel (as one put it), 'I don't see an awful lot of other clergy.' There seemed to be some interest in more mutual support (perhaps through theologically like-minded groups, or through Chapter meetings discussing strategy and survival). Someone remarked that the organisation is 'much more powerful and successful in St James, Piccadilly'.

Chapter meetings seemed to be the focus of the obvious differences between the clergy. '"Racism", "sexism", "police brutality" – they're not representing what people feel . . . You can't actually take somebody from where they're not to where they do not want to be. With the police, you start on the basis we're on the same side.' On the other hand, a clergyman whose fridge had an anti-police sticker on it said of the meetings: 'I approve of what is discussed. But I feel it ought to lead to actions.'

The individualism of the clergy was mentioned: it may be that this is a common factor that underlies the differences. There is 'terrible competitiveness among the Anglican clergy, very built-in'. It was said that the problem was getting people of incumbent status to work in teams. There was evidence of this happening, even though 'theological training [produces] the expectation that people will be running their congregations. Some of this is based on a theological/scriptural model.'

Church attendance and morale

Asked how other clergy reacted to low church attendance, the clergy's responses suggest that in practice this has been the key problem. There is an 'ethos among clergy you don't share failure – you put on a face so that things are better'. (It may be that those opposed to the radical social gospel tend to have larger congregations.) No more than half the clergy were relatively happy about attendance; here it had gone up, generally from very low levels. One clergyman laughed in a pleased-embarrassed way, said there had been an 'increase in numbers, really' and, to be modest, referred to this as a 'miracle'.

Low church attendance is 'depressing'; 'it's been a problem for me'; 'sometimes you wonder what on earth's the good of carrying on'; 'self-esteem' is measured by attendance; 'I sense that under the surface there's a numbers game going on all the time'; there is 'a neurosis about numbers among the clergy'; clergy are 'defensive' about it or 'very sensitive indeed' about it; 'a sense of failure hovers over us'; 'working in the East End is about coping with some sense of failure'; clergy 'always tend to exaggerate' numbers.

The decline in population in Tower Hamlets this century has aggravated an already acute problem. Some congregations seem to be largely white working class, others to have many marginal people.

10

RECOMMENDATIONS

The findings of this research certainly do not make it easy to draw up a convincing strategy for religious agencies, and especially the Church of England, in the East End. The contribution that follows, since the evidence suggests no obvious course of action, is necessarily of a different kind from the analysis so far. The protected purity of the research role does not extend to this final part.

The C. S. Lewis Centre aims both to research in as value-free a way as is possible and to suggest positives in terms of action. In this latter function – though not of course in the analytic processes of 'pure' research – the Centre is committed to the furthering of Christian orthodoxy. The comments that follow combine the insights made possible by my agnosticism with those made possible by the orthodox Christian commitment of the Director, Dr Andrew Walker;[1] his contribution, with which (from my perspective) I agree, is acknowledged by quoting him extensively in what follows.

As a preliminary, the East End and inner city generally need to be seen as special instances of the overall context of 'secularisation'. Much work (not always easy to read) has been done here by sociologists of religion, yet the specialists' sociological understandings of the situation seem to be little appreciated by those who should benefit most, the sorely tried clergy. A thumb-nail sketch follows: a few major references are also given as a starting point in case there is any desire to investigate further.

'Secularisation' in general

Anglicanism in Tower Hamlets and the inner city cannot be divorced from the worldwide processes of 'secularisation'. This is a portmanteau idea[2] which a quite recent theoretical overview[3] has analysed into three conceptually clear sociological aspects.

There is 'laicisation': this French-sounding name labels the position of church religion being pushed to the periphery of modern industrial societies, the traditional sacred cosmos dissolving and rationally orientated, specialised institutions developing. The technical, amoral order of modern society disintegrates the community of pre-industrial society, the local persisting relationships of the relatively stable group.[4] The work of perceiving the different structural ways in which laicisation develops has taken strides recently.[5]

The second aspect of 'secularisation' is religious change: for example, the recent coming into being of cults, or the processes of specialisation and rationalisation within the church themselves. By 1970 as many as a seventh of the actively engaged Anglican clergy were employed in non-parochial, special functions.[6] (Gilbert: 81–95). The third aspect is the nature and extent of individual involvement.

Reversing 'laicisation' in the East End and the inner city

In our culture as a whole, of course, 'laicisation' may prove to be reversible. Historical analogies are generally asserted to be misleading, at least in part; but nevertheless it may be worth mentioning two 'secularisations' that have been followed by great religious and spiritual developments, the times of the later Roman Empire, and those of the Buddha and Mahavira. Very broadly, the latter may prove to be closer than the former to the situation in the West today.[7] The intractable situation in Tower Hamlets and the inner city may well change in the very long term. It is tempting to add, only in the very long term.

Though this intractability may be experienced at its most acute by the Church of England, it is productive of ecumenism since it is also shared by other Christian affiliations. So far as the white working classes are concerned, the problem would appear to be not just a Christian one but also a religious one; but this may not be generalisable to other social groups in Tower Hamlets. Islam may well have much greater relative strength among many immigrant 'working-class' groups, and adapted forms of meditation are available to meet the middle classes increasingly moving into the area.[8]

Particular comments

Television

Here, surely, has been the greatest opportunity for subverting an agency of 'laicisation'. It is difficult to see how religious emotions could ever be stirred on a large scale among the indigenous white working class without effective religious broadcasting. In homes like those of most of the interviewees it seems that the TV is constantly switched on; and though it can only be an interpretative position, it has also been suggested in this research that the invasiveness of the medium has had a considerable influence on the attitudes of the interviewees.

The comment about to be made here extends, of course, far beyond Tower Hamlets and the inner city, and involves policymaking at a high level. A broader, wider Anglican-ism (no doubt rather unrefined and raw) could be con-structed as an 'image'. It has always been true that 'the church cannot hope to man every parish with outstanding men';[9] but professionalism can always be provided for the screen. It is essential, in my opinion, that religious broad-casting stands out in an unembarrassed way as different. Watering down the content by deferring to the very secular atmosphere pervading television studios can attract only diluted commitment. Indications from this research are that Gospel-type services (with largely white participants!) would appeal most to the indigenous white working class, but more research is needed. A successful television pre-sence would make the role of the ordinary vicar easier, since he would increasingly be perceived according to a favourable stereotype conveyed through the legitimacy of the medium. This in turn might have an effect on the small world of scriptwriting.

'Sectarianism' within 'cultural embeddedness'

'Sectarian' options, such as evangelical and charismatic decisions for Christ backed up by the voluntary churchiness of small communities, or the enclave Anglo-Catholicism that has become closely identified with local cultures in the East End, generally are accompanied by more energy and conviction than the broad option of nurturing what Anglican embeddedness remains in an indifferent Tower Hamlets. So sectarian options and cultural embeddedness seem to be widely thought of as alternatives.[10] But the *necessary* conflict between the two is surely small: instead of being 'either/or' the situation can, with admittedly some difficulties, be treated as one of 'both/and'. This is probably the wisest strategy.

Rites de passage

The church shoots itself in the foot with its sectarian retreat into a strict baptism policy. How can theologians answer the roadsweeper (pages 99–100) satisfactorily? If baptism has nothing to do with the grace of God, but is only to do with chosen conscious belief, the baptising of unthinking infants would seem to be pointless. If it is justified as an agent of social conditioning it seems unimportant to *insist* on commitment on the part of one of the parents as a *sine qua non* for the rite to take place: often insistence destroys the prospect of partial social conditioning. It is surely best for discipleship to be somewhat dissociated from baptism policy (even though a very strict policy can lead to increased church attendance). Sectarian impulses can thus foster an increase in commitment without destroying the diffused Anglicanism represented by common, 'imperfect' notions of what baptism is about. The church of the land surely needs to link discipleship to cultural embeddedness; here the *rites de passage* are very significant. In practice, as much commitment as possible could be encouraged from baptism without preventing the rite from taking place.[11]

Financial considerations seemed to be very important to the interviewees in discussing weddings and funerals. It is a pity from the church's point of view that there is no apparent possibility of subverting the agencies of 'laicisation' here, for example, by setting up its own undertaking service.

It has of course often been noted that rite is the last bastion of religion.[12] A sectarian attitude towards access to the rites risks eroding not just orthopraxis but also the Christian mentality which, in however diffused a way, is implicit in the rite.

Evangelical and charismatic commitment

Dr Walker points out that heartfelt religion of the evangelical and charismatic kind may have some success if expertly made available. He comments: 'The Puritanism of New England in the seventeenth century was unable to adapt itself to the Frontier, where there was neither community nor orthodoxy. Methodism and revivalism, however, in going straight for the "heart experience", were able to bypass the problem of religious ignorance and the notion that religion was essentially a "them" religion. Just as black slaves rejected establishment white religion in favour of their own religious forms, so modern East Enders may continue to reject an "Anglicanism" that has never been theirs anyway.' He says, in relation to religious life in the inner city, that 'the battle is being lost on all fronts and in particular at the local church: no longer "my" or "our" church, but simply an archaic building that houses alien rites'.

Dr Walker therefore suggests that 'we need what the social workers call "crisis intervention": teams of laity and clergy who will together break down the rigid barriers between both ecclesiastical and lay structures, and also the no longer viable inner-city parish boundaries'. Also, he proposes that a working party be set up to investigate the methodology and strategy of sects in the inner city. (The research suggests that Jehovah's Witnesses and Mormons have achieved some success in Tower Hamlets.)

Success in evangelising and crisis intervention would only need to be modest to achieve that 'critical mass' that represents a self-sustaining Christian community, rather than a Christian handful. The successive evangelising waves of Methodism, Pentecostalism around the start of this century, and the recent charismatic outbreak, seem to have brought in diminishing numerical returns.

Anglo-Catholicism

This research was not needed to show that, in Tower Hamlets and elsewhere, many clergy will be unable to follow the evangelical and charismatic paths. Dr Walker suggests that Anglo-Catholicism may still have a future. Both approaches – 'low' and 'high' – appeal to the emotions and are not purely intellectualist. Indeed, the cultus of Catholicism (for example, the interest in candles) obviously has an advantage over certain evangelistic approaches, but Dr Walker points out that it will never be more than a minority religion in a world of shifting and declining communities.

The social gospel

Abstract issue-consciousness does not seem to be compatible with the propagation of the Christian gospel and its embeddedness within the white working class. The situation is different with communal involvement and visiting, where the Christian end is fully in mind.

Abstract issue-consciousness

This does not seem to be an effective option for the clergy. Their role uncertainty was being described as perhaps the biggest single problem relating to the social status of the Anglican minister as far back as 1969.[13] Abstract social justice – which, in the form of positive racial discrimination, opposition to the police and denunciation of sexism, is not widely championed by those in whom Anglicanism is most embedded – may appear to give the clergy a role after the general collapse of the voluntary community built up around the Victorian church.[14] But there is nothing specifically Christian about it: indeed, it recalls early 'laicisation' (though with a modern frame of reference).

Visiting

There have been some changes since 1846, when Bishop Blomfield described Bethnal Green as 'the spot where it is said we have sown our seeds in vain': ten churches had been built since 1837.[15] Cockney community was strongly fortified against Anglicanism, apparently more so than rural community. (Keith Thomas has pointed out the likely importance of magic in the supposedly theistic peasant past.) The contemptuous epithet 'cockney', with its likely etymology as one of the small or malformed eggs popularly called 'cock's eggs', suggests the distorting effect of early slum urbanisation. Now, however, this community of deprivation is largely a matter for nostalgia; the main deprivation today is probably a lack of community itself.

This may create a more favourable climate for a visiting clergy[16] with a practical (not abstractly radical) social gospel that is seen and treated as a bridge to Anglicanism, widely defined. The vicar not only seems to create a more positive image for himself by being visible, it also seems that such a policy is likely to lead to some improvement in church attendance. The research suggests that a catalyst for neighbourhood watch schemes that are not perceived as 'them' (e.g., dominated by the police) is overdue. Community is unlikely to be built by encouraging structures, such as tenants associations, whose rationale and ethos belong to 'them'; perhaps the only way it could emerge is through a 'landing' consciousness in which neighbour meets neighbour with a common purpose, such as mutual protection, so that the boundary with the world is extended beyond the front door. This is easy to write about, extraordinarily difficult to achieve.[17]

The option of abandoning orthodoxy altogether in favour of a social solidarity approach has, as Dr Walker says, 'real problems': '(1) There is very little working-class solidarity except in the mind of Marxist theorists. (2) Such a move is really an adaptation to secularism and thus begs the question, "Why have a clergy at all?" (3) If such an approach would ever catch on it would only hasten the demise of the Church of England.'

Church attendance and services

The clergy are victims of 'laicisation' in an advanced stage and also, in the inner city, of the rule that the lower the socio-economic status the more attenuated the practice;[18] in Tower Hamlets they are also the victims of the decline in population, especially since it is the successful who tend to move out.

The liturgy, rite and service that appeal most in Hertfordshire are almost certainly not well adapted to the inner city. An advantage of recent liturgical change is perhaps an increased possibility of flexibility. Down to earth, robust and even bawdy ritual would probably suit the East End white working class best (though such a quasi-medieval touch would no doubt alienate many existing churchgoers). The seventeenth-century ideals of restraint and impersonality are 'them'. Dr Walker wonders whether the recent liturgical changes in the Church of England are 'merely adaptations to middle-class prejudice' that do not speak to the condition of the inner city; he points out that 'the broad, rationalistic, sceptical church (which flourishes among so many middle-class clergy)' is least likely to attract the inner city.

Presentation in these cultural circumstances needs to be expressive. Candles, for example, are 'us' and so a bridge between indifference and what to Anglicans might seem an adequate theism. Probably, the less demure the candles are, the more they will appeal. Variety, simplicity and naturalistic involvement are much more likely to engage the East Ender than doctrine; orthopraxis will probably mean more than orthodoxy.

The research suggests that the reality of suffering (in nature perhaps even more than through social and individual human agency) is a pervasive problem. It also suggests that Jesus as the Son of God has low credibility. There is very little fusion between the two in the idea of salvation through the suffering God. This image or deep thought at the heart of the Christian good news is far from reaching Tower Hamlets. Despite the apparent indifference – or worse – to sermons, it might be worth experimenting conveying the idea of the God who suffered for all through concrete instances of Tower Hamlets-type feeling for suffering.

It is very tempting to suggest that little importance should be attached to church attendance in the inner city. Against this, it needs to be pointed out that attendance is about the only act of communitarian orthopraxis left to the Church of England. Identity may be better preserved by a painful awareness of empty pews than by abandoning services.

Clergy support

Though the clergy know that in very large part the distress so many of them feel in Tower Hamlets and in the inner city is the product of overriding social forces, they would be less than human if they did not react adversely. A paper such as this, written by an outsider, might at least be useful in promoting a full acceptance of the objective nature of these forces.

Strategies to subvert them could include realistic discussion among the clergy themselves of their common plight, not excepting their feelings and emotions. In this situation the in many ways useful culture of clerical competitive individualism has disadvantages. Team work would provide some sort of community for the clergy and might convey to others that the physicians can heal themselves.

The church with its differentiated functions could be instrumental in organising professional support such as counselling for the clergy and their wives and families. Retreats in which tensions are projected through prayer on to Christ, only to return later, are clearly palliatives. More naturalistic and psychologically effective insight should have a major part to play in making service in the inner city an emotionally enriching experience.[19]

NOTES TO PART ONE

Introduction

1 See *Faith in the City, The Report of the Archbishop of Canterbury's Commission on Urban Priority Areas* (Church House Publishing 1985), pp. 65–67. The preface to this report states the terms of reference of the Commission as follows: 'To examine the strengths, insights, problems and needs of the Church's life and mission in Urban Priority Areas and, as a result, to reflect on the challenge which God may be making to Church and Nation: and to make recommendations to appropriate bodies.'
2 The terminology of this subject is complicated; it is discussed more fully in chapter one.
3 Extensive and regular reviews of the literature in the sociology of religion can be found in both *Social Compass* and *Archives de Sciences Sociales des Religions*. Both these bibliographies include studies on the nature of belief. Current research in this country is contained in the Register of the Sociology of Religion Study Group of the British Sociological Association. It would however be foolish to claim that any review of literature is exhaustive; the more so in an area so difficult to define as this one.

Chapter one

1 See, for example, the fifty-three terms listed by Edward Bailey in his doctoral thesis, *Religion of a Secular Society* (unpublished PhD, University of Bristol 1976), note facing p. 189.

2   R. Toon, *Methodological Problems in the Study of Implicit Religion*, The University of Leeds, Department of Sociology, Religious Research Papers, no. 3. See Appendix A for fuller details of the Leeds project. (The Leeds Religious Research Papers will be abbreviated in the notes to RRP followed by the appropriate number.)

3   ibid., p. 9.

4   See R. Towler and A. Chamberlain, 'Common Religion', in M. Hill (ed.), *A Sociological Yearbook of Religion in Britain*, 6 (London 1973), pp. 1–28, and R. Towler, *Homo Religiosus* (London 1974), ch. 8.

5   Towler, *Homo Religiosus*, p. 146; T. Luckmann, *The Invisible Religion* (London 1967).
    Edward Bailey's approach to implicit religion very largely follows Luckmann's. See Appendix B for a fuller discussion of this.

6   Towler, *Homo Religiosus*, p. 148; common religion is contrasted with official religion: 'If by official religion we mean beliefs and practices which are prescribed, regulated and socialized by specialized religious institutions, then common religion may be described as those beliefs and practices of an overtly religious nature which are not under the domination of a prevailing religious institution.'

7   See Leeds RRP, no. 12. A number of recent publications include material on the nature and content of common religion. In addition to the Religious Research Papers published by the Department of Sociology, University of Leeds, we should note in particular: E. Bailey (ed.), *A Workbook in Popular Religion* (Dorchester 1986); J. Habgood, *Church and Nation in a Secular Age* (London 1983), chapter 5; M. P. Hornsby-Smith, R. M. Lee and P. A. Reilly, 'Common religion and Customary religion: a critique and a proposal', *Review of Religious Research*, 26 (3), March 1985; D. Martin, *A Sociology of English Religion* (London 1967); idem., *The Religious and the Secular* (London 1969); B. Reed, *The Dynamics of Religion: Process and Movement in Christian Churches* (London 1978); Towler, *Homo Religiosus*.
    From the United States, much more selectively, I have used: Luckmann, *Invisible Religion*; Gustav Mensching,

'Folk and universal religion', trans. Louis Schneider in Schneider (ed.), *Religion, Culture and Society* (New York 1964); L. Schneider and S. Dornbusch, *Popular Religion: Inspirational Books in America* (Chicago 1958); R. Bellah, 'Civil religion in America', reprinted in Bellah, *Beyond Belief* (New York 1970). I have included Bellah's highly influential essay, though its emphasis is rather different from the idea of common religion as suggested by Towler. With Bellah, the focus lies on the corporate – in this particular case on the American nation – rather than on the beliefs of individual people.

On implicit religion more generally, Edward Bailey has prepared a very full annotated bibliography. For details of this, see Appendix B. In contrast, I have selected only those works most immediately relevant to this paper.

8   A phrase suggested to me by Dr Towler.

9   It is interesting, for example, that the critique of Towler has come from those working with Catholic groups. It may be that Catholic teaching, even when dissociated from Catholic practice, stands out in our culture in a way that 'diluted' Anglicanism or even Protestantism would not. In consequence it becomes easier to distinguish remnants of church-based religion from a folk religion transmitted prior to the socialising influences of the churches. See Hornsby-Smith et al., 'Common religion'. It would be interesting in this respect to look at the parallel of non-practising Protestants within a predominantly Catholic culture.

10   Leeds RRP, no. 11.

11   Studies of folklore: A. W. Smith, 'Popular religion', *Past and Present*, 40, 1968, pp. 181–86; idem., *The Established Church and Popular Religion, 1750–1850* (London 1970).

Historical studies: H. McLeod, *Class and Religion in the Late Victorian City* (London 1974); J. Obelkevich, *Religion and Rural Society* (Oxford 1976); K. Thomas, *Religion and the Decline of Magic* (London 1971); E. P. Thompson, *The Making of the English Working Classes* (Harmondsworth 1968); E. R. Wickham, *Religion and Society in an Industrial City* (London 1957); A. Wilkinson, *The Church of England and the First World War* (London 1978); idem., *Dissent or*

Conform? War, Peace and the English Churches 1900–45 (London 1986).

Cultural studies: R. Hoggart, *The Uses of Literacy* (Harmondsworth 1957); I. and P. Opie, *The Lore and Language of Schoolchildren* (London 1959); G. Gorer, *Exploring English Character* (London 1955); idem., *Death, Grief and Mourning in Contemporary Britain* (London 1965).

Psychological approaches: G. Jahoda, *The Psychology of Superstition* (London 1969).

Anthropological approaches: M. Douglas, *Natural Symbols* (London 1970); E. C. Banfield, *The Moral Basis of a Backward Society* (Illinois 1958); D. Clark, *Between Pulpit and Pew* (Cambridge 1982): this is primarily a sociological book, but uses anthropological techniques of study.

Sociological work: details of these studies will be given as they are referred to in the text.

12 Two of the historical works cited in the previous note stress this point in particular. Keith Thomas' study of magic and religion in the sixteenth and seventeenth centuries, and James Obelkevich's detailed analysis of nineteenth-century rural Lincolnshire both show that even in periods where the official church was strong and confident of its own position, it by no means had a monopoly over people's religious beliefs. Superstition and pagan influences played a very large part in everyday thinking.

13 It was a great pity, for example, that the in-depth interviews planned as part of the Leeds study never in fact took place. Though not strictly speaking participant observation, these would have balanced the more formal survey techniques. See also the discussion at the beginning of Dr Ahern's paper.

14 Clark, *Between Pulpit and Pew*, is an example of participant observation techniques used to the very best advantage.

15 Toxteth is a good example of how this can happen. Very rarely do the religious aspects of this community receive public comment. There are however nearly sixty religious organisations of one kind or another in this relatively small area of Liverpool, without including common religion aspects at all. See *Faith in the City*, p. 45.

Interesting in this respect were Clifford Longley's perceptions about Liverpool in connection with the Heysel football tragedy, 'City with a sense of religion', *The Times*, 10 June 1985. One can only speculate how another city might have reacted if faced with a similar disaster.

16   Martin, *Sociology of English Religion*, p. 52. Gorer, *Exploring English Character*. ABC Television, *Television and Religion* (London 1965); B. L. Laver and B. S. Rowntree, *English Life and Leisure* (London 1951); T. Cauter and J. S. Downham, *The Communication of Ideas* (London 1954); Mass Observation, *Puzzled People* (London 1948); R. J. Silvey, *Religious Broadcasts and the Public* (London 1955).

17   *Puzzled People*, Summary of Conclusions, p. 156.

18   The question of social class differences in relation to religious belief is not always clear cut. The Mass Observation study, however, strongly stresses the lack of influence, which – they say – is peculiar to this subject. See *Puzzled People*, especially p. 79 and p. 82.

19   Gorer, *Exploring English Character*, p. 243.

20   For example, see the introductory paragraphs in chapter 3 of *Puzzled People*, quoted in Martin, *Sociology of English Religion*, p. 53. The chapter is entitled 'The Great Muddle'.

21   R. Towler, Leeds RRP, no. 11, pp. 6–10.

Most of the following are included in the work that Towler himself reviews; I have, however, added one or two related studies to the original list: N. Abercrombie et al., 'Superstition and Religion: the God of the Gaps', in D. Martin and M. Hill (eds), *A Sociological Yearbook of Religion in Britain*, 3 (London 1970). (There are eight volumes of the *Yearbook*, 1968–1975. These contain a number of empirical studies concerning different aspects of the sociology of religion in Britain. They are a useful source of information.) Towler and Chamberlain, 'Common Religion'; G. H. Gallup, *The Gallup International Public Opinion Poll: Great Britain 1937–1975*, 2 vols (New York 1976); B. Martin, 'Comments on some Gallup Poll Statistics', *Sociological Yearbook*, 1 (London 1968): this is a useful summary of the kind of information that it is reasonable to expect from survey material, and at the same time it points out the limitations inherent in such studies. Results are analysed from polls taken between 1963 and 1967. B. Martin and R. Puck, *Young People's Beliefs*, Report to the Board of Education of the Church of England, 1977; M. Staton, *The Rite of Churching: a Sociological Analysis with Special Reference to an Urban Area in Newcastle*, unpublished M. Phil. thesis, Newcastle upon Tyne, 1980; P. Jarvis, 'Towards a Sociological Understanding of Superstition', *Social Compass*, 27, 1980.

22 N. Abercrombie et al., 'Superstition and Religion', p. 124.
23 ibid., p. 106.
24 Examples of the kind of analysis possible with the Leeds material are given in RRP, no. 10, pp. 32–43.
25 Leeds RRP, no. 12 gives the basic frequencies by question to the Interview Schedule. In addition, the Appendix to RRP, no. 10 gives a brief summary of selected results (pp. 47–54).
26 M. Abrams et al., *Values and Social Change in Britain* (London 1985), especially chapter one.

The European Values Study aimed initially to analyse and describe the moral and social value systems prevailing in Europe. The enquiry has since been extended to non-European countries. Reference to the cross-cultural analyses permits a comparative assessment of the British results; for example, with respect to those of the ten commandments which have a moral as distinct from religious reference, the British have – comparatively speaking – a markedly moralistic average score.

27 Leeds RRP, no. 9, p. 17; see also RRP, no. 5.
28 *Media Portrayals of Religion and their Reception*, the final report of a project funded by the Christendom Trust from January 1982 to June 1983 (unpublished paper available from Dr Knott, Department of Theology, University of Leeds). This includes a bibliography on the role of the media in relation to religion. For more information on the significance of the outlook of those responsible for the media, see in particular pp. 70ff.

Chapter two

1 Common religion is an important theme in this debate in

that the persistence of a relatively strong strand of non-institutional religion to some extent at least challenges the theory that our society is becoming progressively more secular.

2   The concept of secularisation is discussed further in the concluding section of Dr Ahern's paper.

3   The argument here is taken in the main from D. Martin, *A General Theory of Secularization* (Oxford 1978).

4   ibid., pp. 28–32. On the contrast in this respect between Britain and America, see also M. Argyle and B. Beit-Hallahmi, *The Social Psychology of Religion* (London 1975).

5   Martin, *General Theory*, p. 32.

6   'Sir Alister's basic thesis is that man's awareness of a power beyond himself is one of the basic drives in his makeup, as natural and undeniable as sex, and possibly the key to man's evolutionary success,' G. Priestland, *The Case against God* (London 1984), p. 70.

The award of the Templeton Prize in 1985 to Sir Alister Hardy was made in recognition of the founding of the Religious Experience Research Unit in Oxford, subsequently renamed the Alister Hardy Research Centre.

David Hay has published a number of books and articles on his work. I have used: *Exploring Inner Space: Scientists and Religious Experience* (Harmondsworth 1982); 'The spiritual experience of the British', *New Society*, 12 April 1979; 'Secular Society/Religious Meanings: a contemporary paradox', published jointly with Ann Morisy in *Review of Religious Research*, 26 (3), March 1985.

7   Hay and Morisy, 'Secular Society', p. 224. It should be added, however, that a question about religious experience in the Leeds survey elicited a much lower response than that found by Hay. On the other hand, this question comes two thirds of the way through the Leeds schedule, when a large number of points that Hay might have picked up had already been dealt with.

8   Martin, *The Religious and the Secular*, p. 107.

Chapter three

1   On the latter point, see, for example, N. Abercrombie et al.,
    'Superstition and Religion', p. 99 and R. Towler in RRP,
    no. 10, p. 48.
2   This sort of difference cuts across the denominational
    boundaries and, within Anglicanism, across different kinds
    of churchmanship. It has a wide application.
3   The Leeds questionnaire does, however, begin to ask ques-
    tions in this area; for example, those relating to a person's
    image of God or of the supernatural: Leeds RRP, no. 12,
    p. 47.
4   E. C. Banfield, *Moral Basis*, p. 130. Other very similar
    examples could be found in C. Levi, *Christ stopped at Eboli*
    (New York 1963), English edition.
5   Leeds RRP, no. 12, p. 47; no. 10, p. 50.
6   A possible example of a change in perception of God that
    results from a change in social advantage comes from a
    memoir of pre-war Liverpool, Helen Forrester, *Twopence
    to cross the Mersey* (London 1981). This is an account of a
    well-to-do family who returned to Liverpool after bank-
    ruptcy and lived more or less destitute in the centre of this
    city. The narrator is the eldest child of the family, a sensitive
    teenager who replies to a question about church
    membership:
    '"We are Church of England," I said. "That is . . ." I
    hesitated. "That is, when we are clean and rich we are
    Church of England. I suppose at present we are nothing"'
    (p. 127).
    And a few pages further on, this contrast is elaborated:
    'The beauty of the language of King James's Version of the
    Bible and of the Church of England Prayer-Book and the
    rich poetry of the hymn-book were not lost upon me, and
    enriched my knowledge of the English tongue.' 'Now, when
    mental stimulus was most required and religious comfort
    desperately needed, these things were gone from us. I
    believed that God was not just angry with us – he was simply
    furious' (p. 132).
    On the whole, the local church comes out of this account
    of pre-war Liverpool fairly well in terms of practical help to a

family in need. The perceptions of a sensitive teenager who, involuntarily, crossed a social divide are, however, illuminating. See also the two subsequent volumes, *Liverpool Miss* (1982) and *By the waters of Liverpool* (1983).

7   The following references are taken from Hugh McLeod's paper 'New Perspectives on Victorian Working Class Religion: The Oral Evidence', *Oral History*, 14 (1), Spring 1986. Though well aware of the difficulties involved with this kind of material, McLeod nonetheless concludes:

> This evidence has changed my own views of later Victorian working class religion, persuading me that the church-going minority was larger than is generally recognised, that more account needs to be taken of the influence of Christianity on those who seldom went to church, and that the decline of the churches was a very gradual and long drawn out process (p. 31).

8   ibid., p. 37.
9   ibid.
10 ibid., p. 32.
11 ibid., pp. 31–2.
12 To some extent McLeod's conclusions are echoed in an unpublished paper by David Durston, 'The Image of God in the Worship of a working class Congregation', Grubb Institute Church Studies Programme, 1980. Though the principal emphasis of this paper is rather different, the material demonstrates once again that God can be seen either as harsh or intimidating or precisely the opposite, that is as the friend who protects you from remote or uncaring authority. In this study it seems that the second picture becomes focused on Jesus, 'the gentle one', as opposed to God, who punishes and judges; in this way the two aspects can be held together rather than becoming alternatives.
13 A. M. Greeley, *The Persistence of Religion* (London 1973).
14 Indeed, each Lancashire town will have its own religious identity and a particular way of expressing this. My point is to stress the diversity rather than to elaborate on individual examples.
15 Clark, *Between Pulpit and Pew*, p. 166. More generally the current debate about rural ministry in the Church of

England questions some of the assumptions made about traditional communities. It seems that the institutional church may be struggling in the countryside almost as much as it is in parts of our cities. See L. J. Francis, *Rural Anglicanism* (London 1985) and A. Russell, *The Country Parish* (London 1986).

16 The question of community (or conversely its collapse) seems to me a crucial one both for the health of social life and as a focus for church life. From the point of view of the former, the evidence conflicts. In this connection, Margaret Simey writes of Toxteth:

> Under such mounting stress as the people of the inner city have had to endure, social values take on a new reality and the delusion of individualism is exposed for the sham it is. Their demonstration of loyalty to the ideal of a caring community in the face of intense pressure to pursue individual interests is a source of inspiration for which I am everlastingly grateful. (M. Simey, *Government by Consent. The Principle and Practice of Accountability in Local Government* (London 1985), p. 44.)

Other commentators are less optimistic; for example, the conclusions drawn by Dr Ahern in connection with his research in East London. From the point of view of the churches, it is interesting that the ACUPA report strongly emphasised this level of action in addition to an awareness of the importance of community life in other respects. See also Wesley Carr's analysis of ministry in *The Priestlike Task* (London 1985) and Durston, 'The Image of God'.

17 In many ways this city has an atypical history from a religious point of view. However, the principle of variety within one conurbation is a general one, even if its particular local nuances vary. To put the same idea in more everyday terms, most professional ministers would agree that every parish 'feels' different.

18 For example, the use of the term 'Protestant' in preference to Church of England or Methodist will tell the observer a good deal about the community in question, and the categories in which its inhabitants think.

19   Moreover, within all these various categories or geographical areas, we should not forget the important differences
between men and women and between old and young; once
again, these cut right across social class differences. For
example, Martin and Puck's study of young people's beliefs
indicates some contrasts in the way that adolescent boys and
girls think about God, despite a predominant impression
that most young people hardly think at all in this respect.
Martin and Puck, *Young People's Beliefs*, pp. 21–6; see also
Argyll and Beit-Hallahmi, *Social Psychology of Religion*,
chs. 4 and 5.

20   Each of these points is a question in its own right; but rather
than enumerate each of these in detail, I want here to stress
the variety of factors involved and how difficult it will be to
disentangle their relative strength when it comes to determining to what degree each has influenced individual or
group attitudes. Examples however can be found in David
Sheppard's *Built as a City* (London 1974) and *Bias to the
Poor* (London 1983), especially chapter 3, and in the 1984
editions of *Christian Action Journal*, which provide on-the-
ground examples of how different experiences of church life
colour people's perspectives.

The question of church buildings perhaps deserves emphasis. Opposition – often vehement – to the closure of a
particular building often comes from those who rarely go to
church; moreover, the resulting bad feeling can lead to all
subsequent overtures on behalf of the church being rejected. 'Insiders' not only find this difficult to understand;
they are faced with impossible financial demands in the
maintenance of underused buildings. The dilemma is a real
one.

21   For an example of this approach, see J. Klein, *Samples from
English Culture*, 2 vols (London 1965).

22   The importance of childhood learning in the acquisition of
religious attitudes is stressed by P. Jarvis in 'Religiosity: a
theoretical analysis of the human response to the problem of
meaning', *Research Bulletin of the Institute for the Study of
Worship and Religious Architecture* (Birmingham 1983).

23   G. K. Chesterton's phrase 'the dumb certainties of existence' encapsulates this very well; hence the difficulties for

the researcher, who inevitably depends to some extent on the ability of people to put into words very deep feelings. See Dr Ahern's introduction for further discussion of this point.

A series of studies carried out in East London by the Stepney Action Research Team (START, Oxford House, Bethnal Green) are also relevant to this question. In particular, a progress report entitled *Images of God in East London* (July 1980) investigates the hypothesis that East London people do have experiences of God, but lack the collective and systematic theology in which to express them; indeed, this lack is seen as one aspect of their deprivation. In addition, see A. Shilling, *The Work of the Evangelist in Inner City areas and on Housing Estates*, Church Army Insight Paper, new series no. 1, 1981. (Sister Shilling was a member of the START team.)

In a rather different context, 'inarticulate religion' and the misunderstanding often associated with it are themes stressed in Alan Wilkinson's study of the First World War, *The Church of England and the First World War*.

24 Basil Bernstein's language theories have received considerable attention, and there is an extensive literature on them. They will be outlined in almost every textbook in the sociology of education.

In *Natural Symbols*, Mary Douglas has taken Bernstein's approach and applied his thinking to the analysis of ritual. In so doing, she sheds new light on patterns of religious behaviour.

A more direct application of Bernstein to liturgy can be found in Douglas Davies, 'Social Groups, Liturgy and Glossolalia', *The Churchman*, 90 (3) July–Sept. 1976, pp. 193–205. This is a perceptive start to an analysis that could be taken much further.

25 For example: P. Jarvis, 'Religious socialization in the Junior School', *Educational Research*, February 1974; M. Hornsby-Smith, *Catholic Education: the unobtrusive partner* (London 1978); M. Hornsby-Smith and R. M. Lee, *Roman Catholic Opinion: a study of Roman Catholics in England and Wales in the 1970s*, (Guildford 1979), especially chapter VI; L. Francis' extensive work on teenagers and

young people, especially 'Denominational Schools and Pupil Attitude Towards Christianity', *British Educational Research Journal*, vol. 12, no. 2, 1986 and *Religion in the Primary School: Partnership between Church and State?*, London, 1987. See also Clifford Longley's comments in *The Times*, 15 September 1986, 'Educating for this world – or the next.'

In addition, we should note Martin, *Sociology of English Religion*, p. 89: 'By a happy chance for Christianity those who teach in primary schools are amongst the most well-disposed to the faith and most strongly practising of all social strata.' More generally, Martin stresses the important role of the female in all aspects of religious socialisation (pp. 125ff. and *The Religious and the Secular*, pp. 111ff.), and suggests that the changing role of women in our society may have a crucial effect in this area.

26 Interesting in this respect are the articles on implicit, common and folk religion in J. M. Sutcliffe (ed.), *A Dictionary of Religious Education* (London 1984). Ninian Smart's entry on implicit religion stresses the importance of relating the teaching of religious education to the immediate experience and cultural world of the pupils. Obviously good RE teaching involves a number of different approaches, but the use of the concept of implicit religion in this context is an interesting step. The issues facing RE teachers in the inner city are of immediate relevance to churches in a similar situation. (See Appendix B for Conferences relating implicit religion to the educational world.)

See also E. Robinson and M. Jackson, *Religion and Values at sixteen plus*, Alister Hardy Research Centre and Christian Education Movement, 1987.

27 Margaret Simey's heartwarming tribute to the churches in Toxteth and their commitment to stand alongside the people rather than against them is a good illustration of personalities overcoming this bias. See 'In my experience . . .', *Christian Action Journal*, Winter 1984, p. 5: 'In the struggle to retrieve for the people from the bureaucracy their right to social responsibility, the local churches have bravely and openly taken their stand on the side of the people.'

Also relevant to this point are Dr Ahern's remarks about

the East London clergy becoming better liked if they are better known. Similarly, the START team found a willingness to accept the individual priest or minister despite a reluctance to be associated with the church as an organisation; see the report *Building an indigenous church in East London* (July 1980).

28 Moreover, the Church of England – and indeed the other churches as well – has a long and specific history as an institution. The consequences of this history, even if regrettable, have to be lived with; they cannot be discarded at will.

29 Leeds, RRP, no. 12, p. 37. Other commentators, however, put a greater stress on only the 'good life', that is on a system of ethics rather than belief; for example, Hoggart, *Uses of Literacy*.

30 Abercrombie et al., 'Superstition and Religion', p. 124.

Chapter four

1 See Towler, *Homo Religiosus*, p. 151. If, to some extent, the problem for the church is becoming more acute in this respect, it is by no means new. See chapter one, note 12 for evidence of the strength of common religion in previous centuries. Moreover, Obelkevich, *Religion and Rural Society*, concludes: 'It is hard to avoid the conclusion that paganism was dominant and Christianity recessive in popular religion. Paganism was rarely Christianized, but Christianity was often paganized' (pp. 305–6).

Douglas Davies, 'Natural and Christian Priesthood in Folk Religiosity', *Anvil*, vol 2, no. 1, 1985, pp. 43–54, is a more contemporary comment on the ambivalent and complex relationship between orthodox and common religion. Central to Davies' discussion is the concept of merit as the prime dogma of folk religion; for example, people ask about suffering in these terms – individuals do or do not deserve what is sent to them. 'The popular concept of merit seems to imply a scheme of *quid pro quo* balance of moral behaviour and success in life' (p. 47). Matching this kind of idea with Christian theology will not always be easy.

2 Indicative of this is the enormous amount of material pro-

duced by the churches on the subject, and in particular on the issues surrounding infant baptism.

The wider question of folk religion and its implications for the churches are discussed in Reed, *Dynamics of Religion*; J. Habgood, *Church and Nation*, in Wesley Carr's two recent books on ministry, *The Priestlike Task* (London 1985) and *Brief Encounters* (London 1985), and in M. Silversides, *Folk Religion: friend or foe?* (Grove Booklets 1986). Shorter contributions are to be found in Bailey (ed.). For full reference see page 135, note 7.

The most sensible policy seems to be one which uses folk religion as a base on which to build, but at the same time stresses the need to 'affirm' selectively; that is, to strengthen those elements that are closest to an authentic Christian faith and to discourage those that are not.

3 The significance of this is even greater if we remember how far into society Sunday schools and other ancillary organisations reached before the first war. See Martin, *Sociology of English Religion*, pp. 41ff.

4 See 'In my experience . . .', *Christian Action Journal*, Winter 1984, p. 20, para. 4/1.

5 On this latter point see Martin, *Sociology of English Religion*, p. 104. In many ways the clergy are expected to be able to articulate. Moreover, this skill can be applied at different levels; for example, a church leader can act as a spokesman for a whole community as well as helping one individual to express himself clearly.

6 This is a point that I discussed at some length with both Edward Bailey and Margaret Simey. Each reached a similar conclusion, though from a very different starting point (see Appendix B). Its significance was underlined by the ACUPA report, *Faith in the City*, p. 66.

7 Once again, Dr Ahern's paper encourages this conclusion. This does not mean that services should be abandoned; rather it encourages other means of outreach alongside more conventional methods.

The lack of a 'fringe' membership in UPA parishes re-inforces this line of thought. If there is no fringe, effective evangelism will have to take place outside the church. See *Faith in the City*, p. 37.

8 Liverpool was one of the first educational authorities to introduce parent governors.

9 For a full discussion of this question within the educational context, see N. Beattie, *Professional Parents* (London 1985), especially pp. 83–7 and 205–12.

10 R. Frankenberg, *Communities in Britain* (Harmondsworth 1966), especially p. 16.

11 This does not imply a rigid application of parish boundaries where these no longer have meaning. It does imply some sort of system whereby the church takes responsibility for every part of our society. Conversely, every individual should be aware of how they can gain access to the church. Even better if they can know the face likely to open the vicarage door, for that, it seems, encourages their coming.

12 The Survey of Clergy commissioned by the Archbishop's Commission gives support to the idea that social conditions in UPA areas depressed clergy more than the difficulties they encountered in their ministry. See *Faith in the City*, chapter two.

13 Indeed, large congregations in the inner city do not always reflect local success; they may well be eclectic congregations gathered from a wide radius. On the other hand, one cannot rule out the possibility of a flourishing working-class church in an urban context; all credit to those who have succeeded in this difficult area, and against all the odds.

Appendix A

1 R. Towler's recent book, *The Need for Certainty. A Sociological Study of Conventional Religion* (London 1984), forms the first part of this project. However, Dr Towler and Dr Knott plan a further volume stressing common religion themes rather than conventional ones; in particular using the Leeds material to look at the kinds of religious variables that are found together in practice, and the personality types with which they are associated.

2 Had the originally planned in-depth interviews taken place, this material would have had even more to offer in that the total reliance on survey technique would have been overcome at least to some extent.

Appendix B

1 Details of these are available from Dr Bailey himself (Winterbourne Rectory, Winterbourne, nr. Bristol). The range of papers offered at these conferences is impressive; a number have been published, though independently of the Network for the Study of Implicit Religion.

2 In particular I have used: *Aspects of Implicit and Civil Religion, a Selection of Readings and References with Introduction and Bibliographical Index.* This provides a very extensive annotated bibliography in the field of implicit religion; it is available from the author.

'The Implicit Religion of Contemporary Society: an orientation and plea for its study', *Religion*, 1983; *'Implicit Religion', and Christian Ministry*, Rural Theology Association Occasional Paper 2, December 1983; 'Civil Religion', 'Common Religion' and 'Folk Religion', in J. M. Sutcliffe (ed.), *Dictionary of Religious Education*; 'Identity as the sacred/holy of contemporary society', *Religion Today. A Journal of Contemporary Religions, 1985*; 'Civil religion in Britain', in H. Kleger and A. Muller, *Religion des Burgers: Zivilreligion in Amerika und Europa*, (Munchen 1985); (ed.) *A Workbook in Popular Religion*; *The Religion of a Secular Society* (unpublished PhD, University of Bristol 1976).

3 From the abstract of Dr Bailey's thesis.

4 The concept of 'integrating foci' runs through Dr Bailey's work to convey what are the principal characteristics of a particular group's implicit religion.

5 Understanding what makes inner city people 'tick' is of course of very great importance to our knowledge of this part of society. It is, however, a far wider question than that envisaged in this paper, and would need very careful definition before any constructive study could come out of it.

6 Martin, *The Religious and the Secular*, p. 108.

Appendix C

1 These are problems encountered by those whose work involves the collection of statistics. Estimations of

membership figures, for example, are bound to be affected by the precise definition given to the term.

An interesting discussion of the meaning of membership (or rather, the variety of possible meanings) can be found in the final chapter of Towler, *Homo Religiosus* (1974), pp. 166ff. The chapter focuses on ecumenism; Dr Towler shows, however, that 'types' of membership may well influence an individual's feeling about the ecumenical debate.

2 Similarly the Protestant minority in France shows quite specific characteristics not shared by Calvinists in other contexts.

For a discussion of the very complex relationships between belief and practice within the Roman Catholic community in this country, see M. P. Hornsby-Smith, *Roman Catholics in England*, Cambridge, 1987, especially chapter 3. For the influence of Irish immigration on estimates of working-class practice among Roman Catholics in England, see chapter 6, especially p. 116.

3 For more detail on this very complex question, see Leeds RRP, no. 6, pp. 6ff.

4 R. Gill's work on the interaction between theology and social structure is relevant to this point, in stressing how each of these variables influences the other. See R. Gill, *The Social Context of Theology* (London 1975), and *Theology and Social Structure* (London 1977).

In addition, the stress, or otherwise, on theological purity – together with its influence on the concept of membership – will be familiar to sociologists in relation to the church–sect distinction. See B. Wilson, *Religion in Sociological Perspective* (Oxford 1982), pp. 89ff.

5 This point was discussed with me by someone with experience of ministering in both the Liverpool inner city and in the suburbs. In the suburb, the 'cost' of church going was relatively low and in consequence there existed within the church a body of people who in a different social area might well have remained outside. In other words, here is the 'fringe'. In terms of active membership – especially those whose commitment went beyond Sunday attendance – the apparent difference in size between the two congregations might well be less than it first appeared.

NOTES TO PART TWO

Chapter five

1   H. McLeod, *Class and Religion in the late Victorian City* (London 1974), p. 104.

2   'I have seen comparable [to Liverpool] experiences in other cities: the East End of London, South East London, Glasgow, the South Bronx, Harlem, the Lower East Side in New York, Pittsburgh's inner city, Redfern and Glebe in Sydney. The details will be different . . .' D. Sheppard, *Bias to the Poor* (London 1983), p. 19.

Paul Harrison says there is something similar – for all their manifest differences – about Brixton, Gateshead, Londonderry, Southampton and inner-city areas in Southall, Swansea, Leicester, Coventry, Birmingham and Hackney: P. Harrison, *Inside the Inner City. Life under the cutting edge* (Harmondsworth 1983), p. 22.

3   This research has only tangential bearing on 'implicit religion' and the debate about it. To some extent it covers 'common religion' (Towler) and 'invisible religion'. In an area such as Tower Hamlets there may not be much of 'an elementary framework of interpretation relating past, present and future experiences', the detachment for which is dependent on reaching 'a certain level of individuation of consciousness and a corresponding command of language' (T. Luckmann, *The Invisible Religion. The problem of religion in modern society* (London 1967), p. 47); at least, not in the strong sense in which this has been measured by Melanie Cottrell and generally found lacking among her middle-class UK respondents (M. Cottrell, 'Invisible religion and the middle class', private paper, August

1979 (now part of an Oxford University DPhil)).

Other studies elsewhere seem to give more support to Luckmann (e.g. R. Machalek and M. Martin, '"Invisible religion": some preliminary evidence', *Journal for the Scientific Study of Religion*, 15 (3)). Luckmann's words should surely be interpreted as part of a brilliant though perhaps flawed essay in philosophical anthropology (see P. Berger, *The Social Reality of Religion* (London 1967), pp. 175–78 for possible difficulties); when put into operation in research much closer definition is needed. It cannot easily be said that Luckmann is 'proved' or 'disproved'. This is also the case with Edward Bailey's empirical finding that 'the outstanding ontological fact is the self . . . It is the outstanding moral value. Indeed, it is sacred' (E. Bailey, 'The Implicit Religion of contemporary society: an orientation and plea for its study', *Religion* January 1985, p. 75). It would be interesting to know what is meant by the 'self': atman, or the inner self, contentment (the need of most of Cottrell's respondents), egotism, integration?

4 Six interviews were indirect, or for background information.

Chapter six

1 A quantitative survey has been carried out (N. Abercrombie et al., 'Superstition and Religion: the God of the Gaps' in D. Martin and M. Hill (eds), *A Sociological Yearbook of Religion in Britain* 3 (London 1970)). An interesting technique of asking subjects for stories has also been employed, but the results have been automatically interpreted from a theological perspective (A. Shilling and D. Stokes, 'Images of God in East London. Progress Report July 1980', typescript from Oxford House, London E2).

2 'White': an Anglo-Burmese of mixed race was included; 'working class' (see I. Reid, *Social Class Differences in Britain* (London 1981)): an unemployed man with seven 'O' levels who said he was from a working-class background and clearly thought of himself as such was included; 'non-churchgoers': attendance at *rites de passage* and very

occasional other services was allowed (otherwise there would have been no quota sample); 'non-Anglican religions': Catholicism, Methodism, etc., were obviously excluded, but a Catholic who said she was Church of England because her husband was included, as was a man who was 'Church of England and Mormon', and those who were 'Christian' or 'Protestant'. (Those who replied they were 'Hebrew' or 'Jewish' were excluded since they seemed to be putting themselves within the ethnicity of Judaic practice. Not belonging to non-Anglican religions of course included those with no religion, agnostics and atheists.)

3 One clergyman with a very strict baptism policy understandably felt it would be a breach of trust to provide me with a list without contacting the people first. His area was (by chance) covered by one of the six recruited through the quota method.

   Another list was exhausted without result (people had moved and one subject was not white working class). Thus two interviews were drawn from a single list.

4 A broad balance was kept between the floors of these (very largely) four to six storey estates. (There were a few tower blocks.) One person was recruited while walking through an estate. One or two people did not live in the estate themselves but had strong connections with it (all lived in Tower Hamlets).

5 Greater precision was not possible on the doorstep since the first names given me did not necessarily correspond with those on the baptism lists, even if the subjects were the same.

6 It was impractical to quantify this. For the purposes of the research it is important to realise that the sample was in effect self-selected. Most refusals were immediate; some talked, teased or hesitated, then refused. Where there was several minutes' doorstep conversation most agreed (an *ex post facto* estimate), but of course very many were not eligible. I usually had to ask to be let inside (two interviews only were held outside the flat of the subject). After the research it was pointed out to me that it is not part of the culture to ask people in.

7 This at least helped me to avert one great fear: that I

was from the Council. (However, many people remained suspicious until well into the interview.) That trust was the real issue was illustrated when I experimented by offering £5 an interview to a few potential quota interviewees. The offer seemed to have a counter-productive effect, except in Bethnal Green.

8 I sensed that on the doorstep in Tower Hamlets there was often an unusually keen awareness of one's less conscious signals.

9 Thus over a year was spent researching the 'religion' of a North Yorkshire fishing village (D. Clark, *Between Pulpit and Pew. Folk religion in a North Yorkshire fishing village* (Cambridge 1982), pp. viii, 35). For a substantive demarcation of the area of 'invisible religion' see R. Toon, 'Methodological problems in the study of implicit religion', *Religious Research Papers*, Department of Sociology, University of Leeds.

10 Selected transcriptions were made.

11 R. Towler and A. Chamberlain, 'Common Religion' in M. Hill (ed.), *A Sociological Yearbook of Religion in Britain* 6 (London 1973), p. 9.

Chapter seven

1 M. Young and P. Willmott, *Family and Kinship in East London* (London 1959), p. 88.

2 J. Harrison, *Attitudes to Bible, God, Church* (London 1983), pp. 8, 47, 71.

3 She asked me for help. I suggested a black Pentecostalist church, and was told that this had indeed been her intention once the transfer was achieved. I suggested she did not wait.

4 B. Bernstein, *Class, Codes and Control* 1 (London 1971).

Chapter eight

1 He found another parson to baptise his child.

2 My working description of 'Anglicanism' in relation to Tower Hamlets is (for the purposes of this research) not

quite the same as David Martin's pinning down of this word in relation to traditional upper middle-class identity (D. Martin, *A Sociology of English Religion* (London 1967), pp. 70–71).

3   Jehovah's Witnesses had obviously visited widely.

4   I did not bring up the subject specifically. For a critique of its identification with occupation, see G. Gorer, *Exploring English Character* (London 1955), p. 36.

5   It is fair to add that a question about historic or old buildings was asked in the context of discussion about the subject's estate.

6   The established church itself may not have this resonance in Wales, for example; this comment is restricted to Tower Hamlets. Robert Bellah's expression 'civil religion' is based on an analysis by Herberg of the 'American Way of Life' as the integrator and validator of United States' social life, taking this legitimising function from what is common in Protestantism, Catholicism and Judaism.

7   Thus clergy in Tower Hamlets have probably been spared scepticism about the triune nature of the Christian godhead.

8   This was disturbing methodologically. I was not aware of giving any signals of expecting a positive answer. (Indeed it is relevant to state that I do not believe in the virgin birth.)

9   The sample may well have under-represented Tower Hamlets white working-class belief in reincarnation. For example, in Europe 21% of Protestants in a recent survey believed in reincarnation (J. Stoetzel, *Europe at the Crossroads* trans. M. James (pre-publication draft summarising the European Values Survey)).

10 'All find safety in the tomb', *Crazy Jane and the Bishop*, W. B. Yeats.

11 Abercrombie et al., 'Superstition and Religion', pp. 100 –101, 120–21.

12 Virtually no one mentioned astrology other than that of the mass media horoscopes. My impression is that really serious astrology in the United Kingdom is largely located among the well-educated upper middle classes.

Chapter nine

1 The interviews lasted on average about one and a half hours.
2 The uncertainty of the clergy in relation to the 'implicit religion' of working-class Tower Hamlets is hardly surprising, since their role precludes the 'anthropological' immersion needed.
3 One Tower Hamlets clergyman refused to cooperate with the research, partly because he saw it as racist for its focus on the indigenous white population. One wonders if he would have said the same if the research (also to cut down variables) had focused on the Bangladeshis.
4 I have also heard this analogy used with conviction to illustrate the 'truth' of reincarnation (Anthroposophical).

Chapter ten

1 Dr Walker was a Research Fellow at King's College, London when this study was undertaken.
2 P. Glasner, *The Sociology of Secularisation, A critique of a concept* (London 1977).
3 K. Dobbelaere, 'Secularisation: A Multi-Dimension Concept', comprising *Current Sociology*, 29 (2), Summer 1981.
4 B. Wilson, *Religion in Sociological Perspective* (Oxford 1982), chapter 6.
5 D. Martin, *A General Theory of Secularization* (Oxford 1978).
6 A. Gilbert, *The Making of Post-Christian Britain* (London 1980), pp. 81–95.
7 Though it is recognised that no cultural situation can replicate itself, the complex phenomenon of the decline of the Roman Empire and the rise of the institutional church may often operate as an implicit model for many hopes for a revived Christianity. But, if analogies are permissible at all, others are possible. About 2,500 years ago the ritualism of the Vedas was yielding during a confused time of social and technological change in which the merging of tribal societies into larger autocratic monarchies coincided with a new iron

technology. Out of philosophical and religious experiment, including philosophical materialism, there emerged the mystical entities of Jainism and Buddhism (and later the Madhyamika, Advaita Vedanta and the Vijnanavada).

Though it is by no means the only significant direction of contemporary religious change, the present tendency towards a diffused mysticism harmonises well with the demands of the new technology today since mysticism is relatively non-institutional and well adapted to a mobile society, is eclectic, and typically appeals to reason rather than faith, to experience rather than to normative absolutism.

8   For example, the London Buddhist Centre in Roman Road, E2, in adopting a personalist approach (the reaction of the pudgalavadins against the general Buddhist teaching of anatta, or the doctrine that there is no self), seems to have adapted Buddhism to the liberal individualist assumptions of the English-speaking middle classes. See Dharmachari Ratnaprabha (J. R. Cooper), 'A re-emergence of Buddhism: the case of the Friends of the Western Buddhist Order', a paper given at the King's College, London, day-seminar on evangelisation and new religions, 14 June 1985.

9   E. Wickham, *Church and People in an Industrial City* (London 1957), p. 265.

10 See D. Martin, 'The Secularization Question', *Theology*, February 1973.

11 The theologically liberal clergy who counterbalance by being strict on social practice probably have a correct instinct: firm boundaries are needed at least somewhere if their churches are to have distinctive identities and so retain congregations. But, for the reasons mentioned, it seems desirable to exempt the *rites de passage* from this strictness.

12 For example, long after the later nineteenth century, when liberal Christian opinion incorrectly persuaded influential Parsis that the dualism in their religion was unhistorical, their rites, descended from the Stone Age through Zoroastrianism, have survived. Obviously of importance to the surival of the rites and meanings of Anglicanism is the future of Church of England schooling.

13 R. Towler, 'The Social Status of the Anglican Minister' in R.

Robertson (ed.), *Sociology of Religion: selected readings* (Harmondsworth 1969), p. 446.

14 Martin, *General Theory*, ch. 7.

15 McLeod, *Class and Religion*, p. 104.

16 There may of course be special problems about visiting for known homosexual, or alcoholic, clergy.

17 NB the practical alliance of compassion between different religious and political groups that is occurring in the inner city (M. Simey, 'The work of the churches in Granby Ward', *Christian Action Journal*, Winter 1984), especially perhaps in areas where the community that is made possible by ethnic boundaries has disintegrated.

18 D. Martin, *A Sociology of English Religion* (London 1967), pp. 15–33.

19 The danger from the church's point of view might be that in some cases a *Liebestod* threatens its institutionality. Indeed, it seems to me that mysticism is more of a threat to orthodox Christian theism in the West than secularism (see note 7 above). I have not mentioned this in the text: for none of the twelve clergy – and only one other 'guardian of the sacred' interviewed – seems to have developed wholly this way, so the relevance to Tower Hamlets Anglicanism in particular seems doubtful. The evangelically minded are perhaps the least susceptible, those with a 'high and dry' consciousness the most. Becoming disillusioned with abstract issue-raising, and so withdrawing affect from it, might lead to the psychological polarisation that is susceptible.

It may be agreed that mysticism, unless it is institutionally induced and contained, is likely to erode Anglican identity, which will be transcended by the directness of intuitive and instinctual realisation. The energy of this may lead people very genuinely into spiritual (or meta-psychological) reductionism: for example, society in its complexity may be interpreted purely in terms of the experience of the foetus in the womb and at birth. Another aspect of the transcendent nature of this insight (however partially true it may be) is the sense that there is salvation in the insight itself, probably because this is not cognitive alone, but is dependent on a path of liberation. For such a psychological gnosis, or uterine utopianism, see D. Wasdell, 'Primal perspective.

Responsive review of *The Secret Life of the Unborn Child* by Dr T. Verney', a privately circulated paper 5 February 1985 (available from URCHIN, 115 Poplar High Street, E14 OAE). (NB the comment in the text about prayer and projection (page 133) was made to me by him.) The typical mistake of such simple – as opposed to sophisticated – mysticisms is surely that they see society as nothing but an aggregation of individuals; for it is over and against the individual, who, in part at least, internalises it willy-nilly. Though of course located in the minds of individuals (one-self and others) society is surely much more emerged and much less permeable than simpleminded mysticism assumes: it is more in accord with the social facts to envisage society as a qualitively discrete entity. Otherwise, mysticism will not abolish the need for society itself, but may well erode a weak aspect of it, e.g., Anglicanism.